GCSE
Geography
for WJEC A

Andy Owen, Cathie Brooks,
Andy Leeder, Glyn Owen & Dirk Sykes

OPTION TOPICS

HODDER
EDUCATION
AN HACHETTE UK COMPANY

Acknowledgements

Text extracts and screenshots

p.11 Extract from St Osyth Parish Council website from *www.stosyth.gov.uk* (October/November 2000); **p.12** *t* Jaywick screenshot from Environment Agency website, *http://maps.environment-agency.gov.uk/wiyby/wiybyController*; **p.15** ' 'Beach war' hotels probed over sand theft' from *Metro* (Friday, 31 July 2009); **p.19** 'Climate change threatens Australia's coastal lifestyle, report warns' from *the Guardian* (27 October 2009); **p.21** *t* 'Safecoast – trends in flood risk', July 2008 from *www.safecoast.org;* **p.24** *br* Screenshot of updated Met Office weather forecast map from *www.metoffice.gov.uk/weather/uk/uk_forecast_weather.html,* © Crown copyright 2010, the Met Office; **p.29** Weather forecast for Snowdonia © Crown copyright 2010, the Met Office; **p.54** *b* Exports of timber from Solomon Islands to China from *www.globaltimber.org.uk;* **p.70** Tourist arrivals to Cancun in Mexico, 2008-09, from Caribbean Tourism Organisation; **p.71** Origin of visitors to Lebanon, June 2009, and Number of visitors to Lebanon (six-months totals from January to June), from Lebanese Tourist Board; **p.73** *t* Map of air transport from *http://epp.eurostat.ec.europa.ed;* © European Communities, 2010, *b* screenshot of Defra's noise mapping website © Crown Copyright; **p.81** Plan of Tyre Coast Reserve from *http://downloaddestinationlebanon.com/destlib/reserves/MAP-inside-TYRE.pdf*; **p.85** Screenshot of South African Tourist Board from *www.southafrica.net/sat/content/en/za/home;* **p.87** Map from Northern Periphery Programme 2007-2013 from *http://www.northernperiphery.eu,* © Nordregio; **p.90** *cl* Screenshot of housing units in Norwich area from *http://rackheatheco-community.com*; **p.94** The Growth of Barcelona, Autonomous Government of Barcelona; **p.95** Extract from *Lonely Planet Guide: Barcelona* by Damien Simonis (Lonely Planet Publications, 2002); **p.103** Barcelona screenshots from *http://w20.bcn.cat:1100/GuiaMap;* **p.106** Extracts from the Primark statement (June 2008); *br* "Primark Kings of Budget Clothing" from *Daily Record* (3 December 2005); **p.109** '£400m giant waste incinerator bid for Ffos-y-fran' by Jackie Bow from *Merthyr Express* (5 February 2009), © Media Wales Ltd; **p.119** Screenshot from *www.poverty.org.uk;* **p.129** 'David Bellamy hits out at North Wales wind farm plans' from *Daily Post* (16 December 2008).

Crown copyright material is reproduced under Class Licence Number CO2P0000060 with the permission of the Controller of HMSO.

Maps on pp. 9, 12, 30, 47, 92, 101, 109 reproduced from Ordnance Survey mapping with the permission of the Controller of HMSO, © Crown copyright. All rights reserved. Licence no. 100036470.

Although every effort has been made to ensure that website addresses are correct at time of going to press, Hodder Education cannot be held responsible for the content of any website mentioned in this book. It is sometimes possible to find a relocated web page by typing in the address of the home page for a website in the URL window of your browser.

Hachette UK's policy is to use papers that are natural, renewable and recyclable products and made from wood grown in sustainable forests. The logging and manufacturing processes are expected to conform to the environmental regulations of the country of origin.

Orders: please contact Bookpoint Ltd, 130 Milton Park, Abingdon, Oxon OX14 4SB. Telephone: (44) 01235 827720. Fax: (44) 01235 400454. Lines are open 9.00–5.00, Monday to Saturday, with a 24-hour message-answering service. Visit our website at www.hoddereducation.co.uk.

© Andy Owen, Cathie Brooks, Andy Leeder, Glyn Owen and Dirk Sykes 2010

First published in 2010 by Hodder Education,
An Hachette UK company,
338 Euston Road,
London NW1 3BH

Impression number   5 4 3 2 1
Year   2014 2013 2012 2011 2010

Cover photo: Kenya, Samburu tribesmen guiding people on camel safari © Gary Cralle/Riser/Getty Images
Illustrations by Art Construction and DC Graphic Design Ltd
Typeset in 10.5pt Trade Gothic by DC Graphic Design Ltd, Swanley Village, Kent
Printed in Italy

A catalogue record for this title is available from the British Library

ISBN: 978 0340 98375 1

Contents

Introduction

GCSE Geography for WJEC Specification A is a new geography course designed for students in England and Wales. The topics that have been selected will help you to make sense of the rapidly changing world in which we live. This book examines current issues that have a life changing impact on millions of people: such as climate change, earthquake hazards, floods, health concerns, globalisation and poverty.

I was thrilled to be asked by WJEC to help structure this new course and I have really enjoyed writing this book. I hope that you will find it useful for your course and that it will inspire you to take a greater interest in a wider study of geography.

Andy Owen

The main features of the book

This book includes some features that have been designed to help you make the most of your course and prepare you for your examinations. These are:

- GIS activities that explain how digital technology is used to store and retrieve geographical information
- advice from one of the examiners, who shows how to get the best mark from common exam questions
- sections in which you are asked to predict what might happen to geography in the future, in 20, 50 or 100 years
- case studies of real places to illustrate the concepts you have studied.

Geographical Information Systems (GIS)

A Geographical Information System (GIS) is a way of storing digital geographical data on a computer or server. Most GIS systems will allow the user to interact with the data to produce a custom-made table, graph or map. Some companies sell GIS programs that will allow you to collect, store and process data on your school's computer system. However, not every school has these programs, so the GIS panels in this book give you the web addresses of some useful GIS sites that are available free on the internet. These sites will allow you to view and process the data that they have collected, but in most cases you cannot add data of your own.

The ability to plan and conduct a geographical enquiry (or investigation) is an essential part of your GCSE. You can use these GIS sites to find geographical data that could help you in your own geographical enquiries.

Examiner's Tips

The examiner's advice panels are designed to help you prepare for standard questions that are asked in the examinations. They have been written by Dirk Sykes, principal examiner for WJEC, responsible for question setting and leading a team of examiners who mark the examinations.

Geography Futures

An exciting recent development in geographical education has been the idea that we should be able to use our understanding of geographical processes and patterns to predict what might happen in the future. This is a particularly important aspect of your course so there are lots of pages in this book devoted to 'Geography Futures'. It makes sense to plan for the future, so Geography Futures pages address issues such as:

- How much will sea levels rise in the future?
- The future of air travel
- Creating sustainable rural communities
- Should we have tidal power in the Severn estuary?

Case studies

A case study is a detailed example of a geographical concept or issue. You will need to learn a few case studies so that you can show in the examinations that you know about real places. You will need to know:

- The name of the place and where in the world your case study is located.
- What the case study is a good example of.
- A few simple facts or figures about the case study.

The location of the case studies (that are outside the UK) are shown on the world map opposite.

Figure 1 The location of case studies (outside the UK) that are used in this book

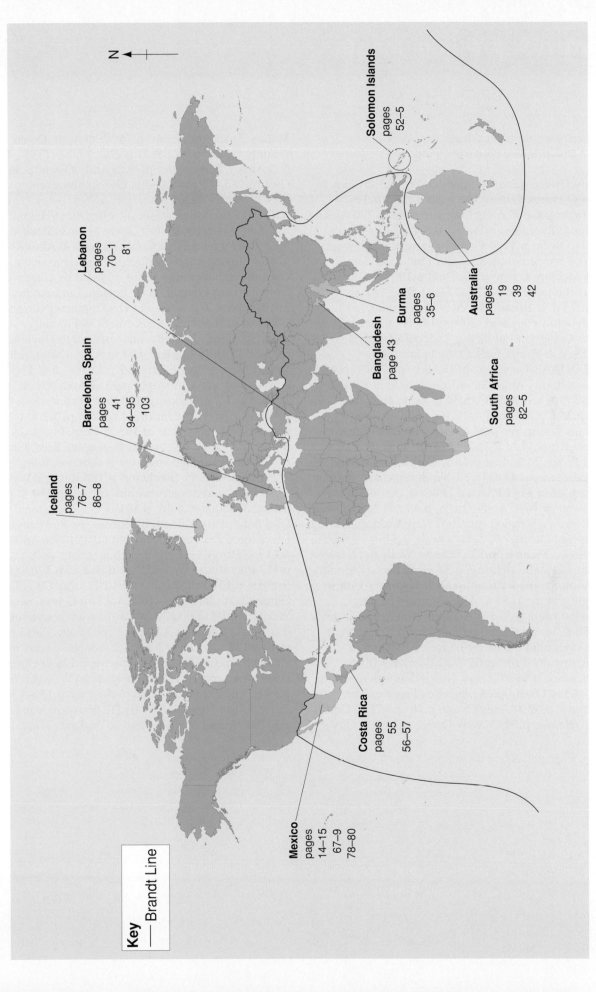

N

Key

—— Brandt Line

Iceland
pages
76–7
86–8

Barcelona, Spain
pages
41
94–95
103

Lebanon
pages
70–1
81

Solomon Islands
pages
52–5

Burma
pages
35–6

Bangladesh
page 43

Australia
pages
19
39
42

South Africa
pages
82–5

Mexico
pages
14–15
67–9
78–80

Costa Rica
pages
55
56–57

Photo acknowledgements

The publishers would like to thank the following for permission to reproduce copyright material:

p.1 © Andy Owen; **p.2** all © Andy Owen; **p.3** © Andy Owen; **p.4** © Patryk Galka/iStockphoto.com; **p.5** all © Andy Owen; **p.6** b © Andy Owen, tr and tl **p.7** © Alamy/Jeremy Moore/PhotolibraryWales; **p.8** © Andy Owen; **p.9** © Andy Owen; **p.11** © Getty Images/Jason Hawkes; **p.13** © GeoPerspectives; **p.15** © PA Photos/AP/Israel Leal; **p.16** © Andy Owen; **p.17** tl and **p.19** tl © Oliver Malms/iStockphoto.com; **p.20** © Getty Images/Jason Hawkes; **p.23** tl © Britain On View/VisitBritain, tr © Purestock/photolibrary.com, 2009, bl © Fotolia.com/Paul Murphy, br © Ingram Publishing Ltd; **p.24** l © Andy Owen; **p.25** bl © Patryk Galka/iStockphoto.com; **p.26** © NEODAAS/University of Dundee; **p.27** bl © NASA; **p.29** © PhotolibraryWales/Steve Lewis; **p.30** bl © Glyn Owen; **p.32** © NASA/GSFC; **p.34** © Getty Images/David Goddard; **p.36** © Corbis/EPA/Yu Riq; **p.37** © Getty Images/Frans Lemmens; **p.38** © Getty Images/Richard Martin-Roberts; **p.39** bl NASA MODIS Aqua, br © Getty Images/AFP/Aris Messinis; **p.43** © Corbis/Tiziana and Gianni Baldizzone; **p.44** © Eye Ubiquitous/Mark Newham/Hutchison; **p.45** tr © FLPA/Paul Hobson, all others © Andy Owen; **p.46** © Andy Owen; **p.48** t © Andy Owen, c © Jef Maion/www.maion.com, b © NHPA/Martin Harvey; **p.50** l © Jacqui Owen, r © Andy Owen; **p.51** © FLPA/Tui De Roy/Minden Pictures; **p.52** © Corbis/Wolfgang Kaehler; **p.53** © Panos/Natalie Behring; **p.54** all © Forests Monitor; **p.55** © Panos/Natalie Behring; **p.56** © NASA/Goddard Space Flight Centre; **p.57** © Alamy/Celia Mannings; **p.58** © Andy Owen; **p.59** t © Alamy/KBImages, b © Andy Owen; **p.60** © Jacqui Owen; **p.63** © Photolibrary.com/CC Lockwood; **p.64** l © Getty Images/Ben Cranke, r © Corbis/Royalty-Free; **p.65** © FLPA/Gerry Ellis/Minden Pictures; **p.66** © Patryk Galka/iStockphoto.com; **p.67** all © Andy Owen; **p.68** all © Rex Features/The Travel Library; **p.69** © Andy Owen; **p.70** and **71** © Corbis/Paule Seux/Hemis; **p.72** © Andy Owen; **p.74** tl © Oliver Malms/iStockphoto.com; **p.76** all © Andy Owen; **p.77** all © Andy Owen; **p.78** t © Thin Black Lines (Tide, 1988), b © Alamy/Travelwide; **p.79** © Andy Owen; **p.80** © Andy Owen; **p.83** © Patryk Galka/iStockphoto.com; **p.84** © Alamy/Stuart Abraham; **p.86** © Andy Owen; **p.87** t © Rex Features/SplashDownDirect/Heimir Harar, c © Andy Owen; **p.88** tl © Oliver Malms/iStockphoto.com, tr © Still Pictures/Nick Cobbing; **p.89** © Andy Owen; **p.90** tl Photograph reproduced with permission Chapelfield Shopping Centre, bl Used by courtesy of Norwich City Council, cr X-Leisure Limited, br Environment, Transport and Development/Norfolk County Council; **p.91** tl © So-Shan Au, bl © Fotolia, cr Alamy/PhotoSpin, Inc., br Getty Images/George Doyle/Stockdisc; **p.92** all © Andy Leeder; **p.94** © Andy Owen; **p.95** tl © Andy Owen, tr Rex Features/Kevin Foy, b © Photolibrary.com/Buckstegen Christoph; **p.98** © Andy Owen; **p.99** logo © All The Little Shops; **p.100** Rex Features/Ray Tang; **p.101** Rex Features/Dimitris Legakis; **p.102** © Patryk Galka/iStockphoto.com; **p.105** © Getty Images/AFP/Simon Maina; **p.106** tl © Corbis/Sophie Elbaz/Sygma, bl War On Want logo from www.waronwant.org; **p.107** all © PA Photos/Barry Batchelor; **p.108** Recycle Wales logo from www.wasteawareneswales.org.uk; **p.110** © Patryk Galka/iStockphoto.com; **p.111** tr Go Wales logo, l © PhotolibraryWales/Jeff Morgan, bc © Alamy/David Levenson, r © Crown copyright (2010) Visit Wales; **p.115** © Patryk Galka/iStockphoto.com; **p.117** PhotolibraryWales/Adrian Beese; **p.120** © Cathie Brooks; **p.121** tr © Really Welsh Trading Co., c Indoor Climbing at Llangorse Multi Activity Centre, near Brecon, Wales. Tel: 0333 600 20 20. Web: www.activityuk.com, b © Cathie Brooks; **p.122** © Oliver Malms/iStockphoto.com; **p.124** tl © Oliver Malms/iStockphoto.com, br iStockphoto.com/Andrey Prokhorov; **p.126** © Oliver Malms/iStockphoto.com; **p.129** © PhotolibraryWales/David Angel; **p.130** tl Oliver Malms/iStockphoto.com; **p.130–1** main image © The Times and 27.01.2010/nisyndication.com; **p.132** © James Lees/Wildfowl & Wetlands Trust.

What are coastal processes and what landforms do they create?

Figure 1 The coastline at Vik, southern Iceland

Activity

1   Study Figure 1.
    a) Describe the landforms that you can see at A and B.
    b) Suggest what processes may be operating at A, B, C and D.

2   Vik beach has been voted as one of the world's top 10 beaches. Discuss the following ideas:
    a) What makes one beach better than another?
    b) This landscape has been used in TV adverts. How would you use this landscape in an advert or film?
    c) About 60 per cent of Wales' population live at or near the coast. List the possible advantages and disadvantages of living near the coast.

What processes are associated with the sea?

Waves provide the force that shapes our coastline. Waves are created by friction between wind and the surface of the sea. Stronger winds make bigger waves. Large waves also need time and space in which to develop. So larger waves need the wind to blow for a long time over a large surface area of water. The distance over which a wave has developed is known as **fetch**, so the largest waves need strong winds and a long fetch.

The water in a wave moves in a circular motion. A lot of energy is spent moving the water up and down. So waves in deep water have little energy to erode a coastline. However, as a wave enters shallow water near the shore its motion changes. The water below the surface is slowed by friction with the sea bed while the water at the surface surges forward freely. It is this forward motion of the breaking wave that causes **erosion**.

Activity

1 Make a copy of Figure 2 and add the following labels in appropriate places.
- Waves in deeper water
- Circular motion
- Breaking wave
- Water thrown forward
- Friction with the sea bed

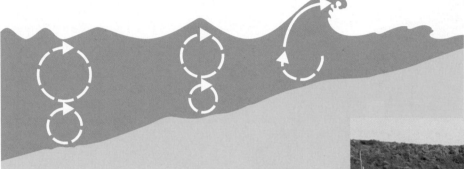

Figure 2 The motion of water in a wave

Processes of coastal erosion

Every litre of water has a mass of 1 kilogram. So a wave containing 2,000 litres (a relatively small wave) will have a mass of 2 tonnes which is similar to the weight of a large family car. The repeated pounding of large waves at the foot of a cliff can cause enormous damage through the process of **hydraulic action**. The repeated hammering effect of the waves on this narrow zone creates a **wave-cut notch**. Cliffs that are already weakened by joints or cracks can collapse and the top of the cliff **retreats** inland. Coastal retreat is particularly rapid on sections of the North Sea coast of England. On some sections of coastline here cliffs are retreating at an average of 2 m a year. The **wave-cut platform** in Figure 3 has been formed by the gradual retreat of the cliffs.

vertical joints in the wave-cut platform

pothole

Figure 3 The rocky shore of the Glamorgan Heritage Coast

Erosional processes

Hydraulic action – waves crash against the cliff, compressing the water and air into cracks and forcing the rocks apart.

Abrasion – waves pick up rocks from the sea bed or beach and smash them against the cliffs.

Corrosion – minerals such as calcium carbonate (the main part of chalk and limestone rocks) are slowly dissolved in sea water.

Attrition – sand and pebbles are picked up by the sea and smash against one another, wearing them down into smaller and more rounded particles.

Figure 4 Four processes of coastal erosion

A huge mass of rocks overhang the notch. This will be the next section of cliff to collapse.

Horizontal bedding planes and vertical joints in the rock are lines of weakness that can be eroded rapidly by hydraulic action.

A recent rock fall. This debris will break the force of the waves so, for a while at least, the cliff behind will be protected from the battering of the waves.

Waves use pebbles from the beach to erode a notch at the foot of the cliff through the process of abrasion.

Figure 5 Evidence of erosion in cliffs on the Glamorgan Heritage Coast

On a map, the blue line showing the coastline of the UK looks like a fixed and permanent feature. In reality, the coastline is a constantly changing environment. Sometimes, battered by storms, it can change overnight with the erosion of tonnes of beach material or the collapse of a massive section of cliff.

Activity

2 Study Figures 3 and 4.
   a) Use the correct erosion terms to complete the annotations below.
   Joints in the rock are widened in the process of … which is when …
   Boulders on the beach are rounded because …
   This pothole has been scoured into the rock by …
   b) Make a simple sketch of Figure 3 and add your annotations.

3 Discuss Figure 5 and its annotations.
   a) Write a list (or draw a timeline) that puts the events acting on this cliff in the correct sequence.
   b) Make another list (or timeline) suggesting what will happen to this cliff in the next few years.
   c) Over the next 100 years this coastline will retreat by about 20–40 m. Draw a series of simple diagrams to show how this process of retreat creates the rocky wave-cut platform in front of the cliff.

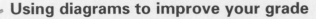

Examiner's Tips

Using diagrams to improve your grade

Geography is a very visual subject and being able to draw good-quality diagrams and sketch maps is an important geographical skill. In the examination you may be asked to include a diagram as part of your answer and the examiner will be impressed by a clear, accurate, detailed and labelled diagram. Diagrams and sketches need to be clear and highlight important features. Labelling and annotation will help describe and explain the important geographical features.

Annotation and labelling

Annotate is a command word which demands that you add explanatory notes. It is more than *labelling* which only requires one word or a short phrase.

Student answer 1

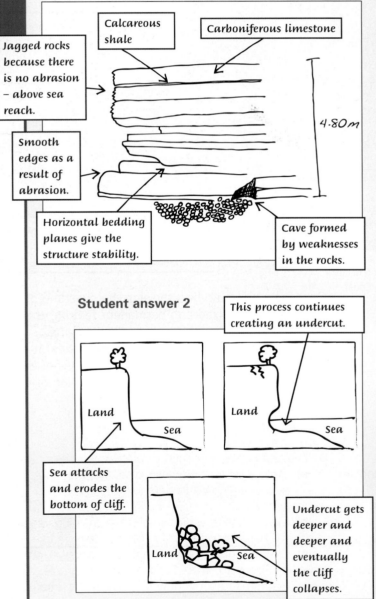

Calcareous shale

Carboniferous limestone

Jagged rocks because there is no abrasion – above sea reach.

Smooth edges as a result of abrasion.

Horizontal bedding planes give the structure stability.

Cave formed by weaknesses in the rocks.

4.80m

Student answer 2

This process continues creating an undercut.

Land

Sea

Land

Sea

Sea attacks and erodes the bottom of cliff.

Land

Sea

Undercut gets deeper and deeper and eventually the cliff collapses.

Sample question

Draw annotated diagrams to describe and explain how the nature of the rock and processes of erosion lead to changes in the position of a sea cliff over time. [6]

What the examiner has to say!

Drawing a good field sketch

Answer 1 is a good-quality field sketch. It is neat, detailed and the annotation is clear although it lacks detail, for example the candidate could have explained how shale is a softer rock and more easily eroded, hence the cliff profile has blocks of more resistant limestone which 'stick out' and the profile therefore appears stepped. (The sketch was made on the Glamorgan Heritage Coastline.)

The diagrams in answer 2 are clear and show progression over time. However, they could be improved by including detail on the nature of the rock, as demanded in the question, for example horizontal bedding. The annotation lacks detail and is descriptive rather than explanatory. It could be improved by adding detail, e.g. in diagram 1 the candidate could explain that the sea attacks the cliff between high and low tide and it erodes through the processes of abrasion and hydraulic action. This answer is worth 4 marks, level 2.

Mark Scheme

Level One (1–2 marks) Diagrams may be limited in quality. Annotation may be mainly descriptive and demonstrates limited understanding. Limited explanation of processes.

Level Two (3–4 marks) Clear diagrams. Annotation demonstrates understanding of the changes in a sea cliff over time. Processes may be identified although not fully explained.

Level Three (5–6 marks) Clear diagrams with detail. Annotation demonstrates understanding of how both the nature of rocks and processes of erosion change the position of the sea cliff. Clear explanation of processes.

Cliffs made of softer rocks and clays have been easily eroded

What remains of a narrow band of very resistant limestone

Figure 6 A cove on the Jurassic coastline of Dorset

Exam practice

1 Imagine you are visiting the Jurassic coastline of Dorset. Complete a field sketch of the photograph in Figure 6. Annotate your field sketch using your own words to explain the processes that led to the formation of the cove in the photograph. Two labels have been added to help you begin this task. [6]

2 Study Figure 7.
   a) Identify and label the following landforms on Figure 7:
   sea cliff, beach, headland, stack. [4]
   b) Annotate the photograph to describe and explain how processes of erosion may lead to changes in the headland over time. [4]

3 With the help of labelled diagrams, explain how different processes and the nature of rocks contribute to the formation of bays and headlands. [6]

Figure 7 Headlands, bays and stacks in the Aolian Islands, Italy

Beach and sand dune processes

Beaches are dynamic environments. In other words, the energy of the wind and waves is constantly moving sediment around and changing the shape of the beach. Where the waves approach the beach at an angle, some of the sediment is transported along the coastline in a process known as **longshore drift**. However, most sediment is simply moved up and down the beach. Each wave transports sediment up the beach in the **swash** and back down again in the **backwash**. All of this movement uses a lot of the wave's energy, so a wide, thick beach is a good natural defence against coastal erosion.

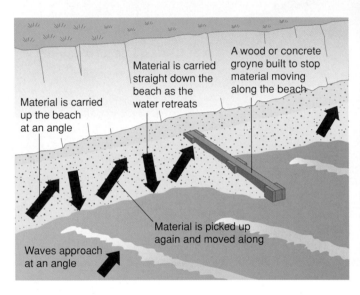

Material is carried straight down the beach as the water retreats

A wood or concrete groyne built to stop material moving along the beach

Material is carried up the beach at an angle

Material is picked up again and moved along

Waves approach at an angle

Figure 8 Sediment transport by the process of longshore drift

Figure 9 The beach at Borth seen from the cliffs to the south of the pebble ridge

| Borth | Case study of sediment movement at Borth on the Ceredigion coast |

The sand and pebbles on a beach usually come from the local environment. Neighbouring cliffs may supply some sediment if they are being actively eroded by wave action. A lot of finer silts and sands are brought down to the coast by rivers. This sediment is then **deposited** in the estuary or on an **offshore bar** at the mouth of the river. It will be washed onshore by the swash of the waves and deposited on the beach.

At Borth, on the Ceredigion coast, there is a pebble ridge making a **spit** on the southern side of the estuary. These pebbles came from cliffs to the south. Figure 9 shows the processes that are supplying and transporting material on this coastline.

Figure 10 The sand dunes at Ynyslas seen from Aberdyfi on the north side of the Dyfi estuary

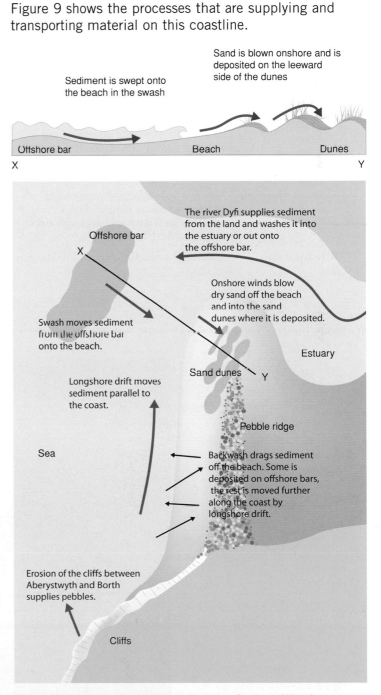

Figure 11 The transport of beach sediment at Borth and Ynyslas on the Ceredigion coast

Activity

1 Describe the landforms seen at A, B and C on Figures 9 and 10.

2 Study Figures 8, 9 and 11. Use an annotated diagram to explain the formation of the pebble ridge on which the village of Borth is built.

3 Study Figures 10 and 11. Make a sketch of Figure 10. Annotate it to explain the processes that have formed the sand dunes at C.

How are coasts managed?

Shoreline Management Plans

Coastal communities expect the government to help protect them from erosion and coastal floods. However, managing the coastline is very expensive. Furthermore, there is no legal duty for the government to build coastal defences to protect people or their property. It is the responsibility of the local councils of England and Wales to prepare a **Shoreline Management Plan (SMP)** for their section of coast. In deciding whether or not to build new coastal defences (or repair old ones) the local council needs to weigh up the benefits of building the defences against the costs. They may consider factors such as:

- How many people are threatened by erosion and what is their property worth?
- How much would it cost to replace infrastructure such as roads or railway lines if they were washed away?
- Are there historic or natural features that should be conserved? Do these features have an economic value, for example by attracting tourists to the area?

Option	Description	Comment
Do nothing	Do nothing and allow gradual erosion.	This is an option if the land has a lower value than the cost of building sea defences, which can be very expensive.
Hold the line	Use hard engineering such as timber or rock groynes and concrete sea walls to protect the coastline, or add extra sand to a beach to make it more effective at absorbing wave energy.	Sea walls cost about £6,000 per metre to build. Sea-level rise means that such defences need to be constantly maintained, and will eventually need to be replaced with larger structures. For this reason hard engineering is usually only used where the land that is being protected is particularly valuable.
Retreat the line	Punch a hole in an existing coastal defence to allow land to flood naturally between low and high tide (the intertidal zone).	Sand dunes and salt marshes provide a natural barrier to flooding and help to absorb wave energy. They adapt naturally to changing sea levels through a process of erosion at the seaward side and deposition further inland.
Advance the line	Build new coastal defences further out to sea.	This requires a huge engineering project and would be the most expensive option. The advantage would be that new, flat land would be available that could be used as a port or airport facility.

Figure 12 The options available to local councils when they prepare a Shoreline Management Plan

Activity

1 Use Figures 13 and 14.
   a) Describe these structures.
   b) Explain how they have helped to protect Borth from erosion and flooding.

Figure 13 Wooden groynes on Borth beach

Management at Borth, Ceredigion

The village of Borth is built on the southern end of a pebble ridge, or spit, that sticks out into the Dyfi estuary. Sand is trapped on the beach by wooden groynes. The sand absorbs wave energy and prevents waves from eroding the pebble ridge. However, the groynes are in poor condition and are at the end of their working lives. What should be done?

The Ceredigion SMP divides the coast up into small Management Units (MU). Figure 15 shows the extent of five of these MUs.

Figure 14 The wooden sea wall at the top of the pebble ridge

Activity

2 Work in pairs.
   Use Figure 15 to provide map evidence which suggests that this coast is worth protecting. Copy and complete the table below and add at least five more pieces of evidence.

MU	
16.2	Railway station at 609901 would be expensive to replace
16.3	
16.4	The campsite at 6192 provides local jobs
17.1	

3 Read Figure 12 carefully. Decide which option you would choose for MU16.2.

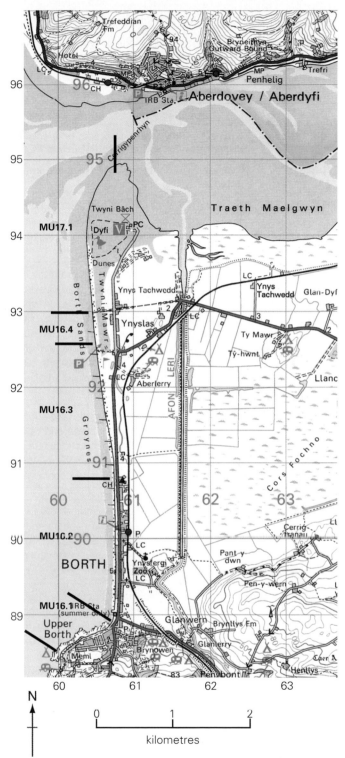

Figure 15 An Ordnance Survey extract of Borth. Scale 1:50,000 Sheet 135

What coastal management is appropriate for Borth?

Ceredigion council decided that there were two possible options for MU16.2 that needed further consideration. Read the points of view in Figure 17 before deciding what you would do.

Do nothing	Loss of property and economic loss in the short term. Change to Borth Bog.	Consider further
Hold the line	Current policy which protects property and businesses. Coastal processes disrupted with reduced longshore drift.	Consider further
Retreat	Retreat would affect homes that are immediately behind the existing line of defence.	Not considered further
Advance	No need to advance the line except to improve the tourist facilities.	Not considered further

Figure 16 The initial decision of the Ceredigion Council for MU16.2

Sand from the southern end of the beach is gradually being eroded by longshore drift, moving it northwards. This process is happening faster than new sand is being deposited. The beach is getting thinner and is less able to protect the pebble ridge (on which Borth is built) from erosion. If the council does nothing then the pebble ridge will be breached by storm waves and the town of Borth, and Borth Bog (Cors Fochno) will be flooded by the sea. This could happen in the next 10 to 15 years. The peat bog at Cors Fochno will be covered in sea water at high tide and its existing ecosystem lost.
Over the next few years erosion will punch more holes through the pebble ridge. A new spit of pebbles will eventually form further to the east. The sand dunes at Ynyslas will probably be cut off and form a small island.

Scientist

The beach and landscape of the spit, including the sand dunes at Ynyslas, are an important economic asset to the village. It's this natural environment that attracts thousands of holidaymakers each year. If the council does nothing then my home and many others will be flooded and local people will lose their livelihoods.

B&B owner

The peat bog at Cors Fochno should be protected from flooding. It is a nationally and internationally important ecosystem. It has protection as a Special Area of Conservation and is also recognised by UNESCO. 'Do nothing' is an unacceptable option.

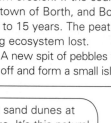

Scientist

We calculate that property in Borth village is worth £10.75 million. On top of this there are many local businesses which would lose their income from tourism if we do nothing. The cost of holding the line is around £7 million. However, we are concerned that building new groynes will prevent longshore drift. We need to consider the impact of that. Currently the sediment moves to Ynyslas where it provides a natural defence to the whole estuary (including the larger village of Aberdyfi) from south-westerly storms.

Local councillor

Figure 17 Views on the future management of MU16.2

Activity

1 Working in pairs, read Figure 17 before completing a copy of this table.

	Do nothing	Hold the line
Economic impacts		
Social impacts		
Environmental impacts		

2 State which option you would recommend. Explain why you think your option is best for this stretch of coast.

3 Would you have made a different decision for MU16.3 or 17.1? Explain which management option might be worth considering for each of these stretches of coastline.

Essex

Managing the coastal flood risk: a case study in Essex

Jaywick is a seaside town in Essex. The flat land here has been flooded by the sea several times. The worst occasion was in January 1953 when 37 people were drowned during a **storm surge**. Low pressure in the atmosphere has a dramatic affect at sea. As air pressure drops during a storm, sea levels rise in a huge bulge known as a storm surge.

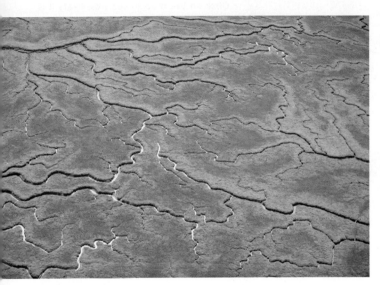

Figure 18 Salt marshes seen from the air. This is the type of environment that is found in grid square 0913 in Figure 23.

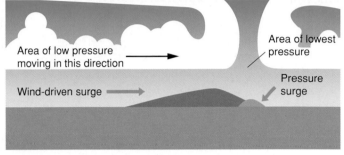

Area of low pressure moving in this direction

Area of lowest pressure

Wind-driven surge

Pressure surge

Figure 19 Storm surge due to low pressure

A great deal of the land edging the parish is composed of salt marsh and mudflats, which have been a natural flood plain for centuries. As development has taken place so properties have been built in these flood plains without much thought to what might happen if the sea rose abnormally. Such an event occurred January 31st—February 1st 1953, the worst weather event of the last century. A combination of a predicted high tide with a deep low pressure area moving south east from Iceland into the North Sea and a storm surge hit the coast, first Scotland then of eastern England. Over 1,000 miles of coastline was flooded, over 30,000 people had to be evacuated from their homes and 307 people lost their lives. In Essex alone nearly 50,000 acres of land were flooded and 113 people died.

Jaywick, which had over 1,700 chalet bungalows, of which over 200 were thought to be occupied, was worst hit. The sea wall was broken in 22 places along our bank of the Colne Estuary and water swept around across St Osyth marshes to the back of Jaywick, a direction from which water was not expected, only to be made worse by yet more breaks in the bank along St Osyth Beach. 35 people were drowned in Jaywick. In Point Clear the two people who ran the grocery store in the Bay were also tragically drowned.

Figure 20 An extract from the St Osyth local government website describing the flood of 1953

Figure 21 Predicted sea-level rise at Jaywick

Year	2007	2032	2057	2082	2107
Rise in sea level (cm)	0	13	35	65	102

Activity

4 Use Figure 19 to give two explanations for the rise in sea level during a storm surge.

5 Use Figure 21 to draw a graph of the predicted sea-level rise at Jaywick.

6 Imagine that you live in Jaywick. Read Figure 20. Given that a lot of land is salt marsh and mudflats, is it sensible for people to continue to live here? Summarise the arguments for each of the following coastal management strategies:
   a) Holding the line
   b) Retreating the line.

Coastal management at Jaywick

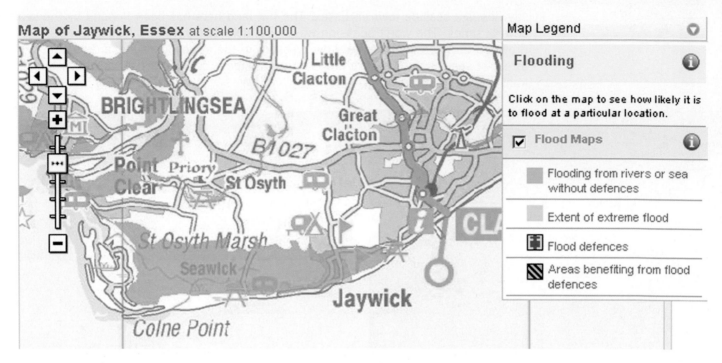

Figure 22 A screenshot from the Environment Agency website showing areas close to Jaywick that are at risk of coastal flooding

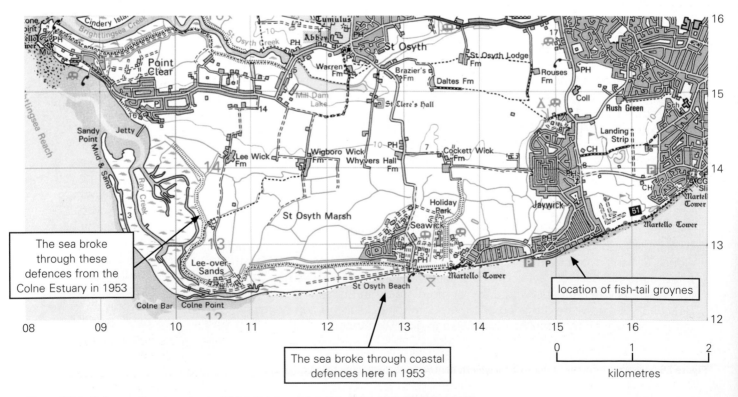

The sea broke through these defences from the Colne Estuary in 1953

The sea broke through coastal defences here in 1953

location of fish-tail groynes

Figure 23 An Ordnance Survey extract of Colne Point and Jaywick. Scale 1:50,000 Sheet 169

Fish-tail groynes

Artificial reef

B

C

Figure 24 An aerial photograph of Jaywick and two breakwaters

Since 1953 the sea defences at Jaywick have had to be strengthened several times. Continual erosion of sand from the beach leaves the sea wall with little protection and it is attacked by pebbles that are thrown against it in the waves (the process of abrasion). In recent years coastal erosion has been managed using both **hard** and **soft engineering** techniques. Hard engineering is the use of artificial structures such as **sea walls** and **breakwaters** to slow erosion or prevent flooding. Soft engineering is the use of natural materials such as sand which replace sediment eroded from the beach.

Two differently shaped breakwaters can be seen in Figure 24. Another breakwater was added in 2009. The breakwaters are built using blocks of granite from Sweden. Each rock weighs 6–8 tonnes so is too heavy to be eroded by wave action. They are designed to slow down the waves and encourage deposition of sand between the breakwater and the beach. They also slow down the rate of longshore drift, but do not prevent it. In the latest scheme, 250,000 tonnes of sand were sucked up from an offshore sand bar, pumped through pipes and onto the beach. The whole scheme cost £10 million and protects 2,600 properties. It should prevent a flood of 4.1 m above normal sea level. This is the kind of flood that is caused by low air pressure and massive waves. A flood of this size could occur, on average, once in every 200 years.

Activity

1 Describe the relief shown on Figure 23.

2 Most of the deaths in 1953 were in the Broadlands housing estate at B (Figure 24). Use the OS map extract to give a grid reference for this area.

3 Compare the width of the beach at C on the map and photo. What does this suggest about the success or otherwise of the hard engineering?

4 Use Figures 22 and 23 to identify settlements that are at risk of coastal floods.

5 Use evidence from Figures 20, 22, 23 and 24 to draw a sketch map of Jaywick and the area flooded in 1953. Annotate it to show where the flood came from, the areas it covered and why it spread so quickly.

6 **a)** Use evidence from the OS map and Figure 24 to state the direction of longshore drift.
   b) Suggest how the breakwaters at Jaywick might affect coastal processes at Colne Point.

7 Make a sketch of Figure 24. Annotate it to show how the coastal management scheme protects this stretch of coastline.

Managing the beach at Cancun

The Mexican resort of Cancun is built on a long, thin barrier of sand in the north-east of the Yucatan peninsula. Like other long spits and **tombolos**, the Cancun–Nizuc barrier was formed by the process of longshore drift which transports sediment parallel to the coast. The white sandy beach is a major tourist attraction. It also helps to absorb wave energy and protect the resort from storm surges. It therefore needs careful management.

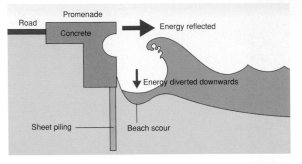

Figure 25 Badly designed sea walls can cause erosion of the beach

Cancun's beach was severely eroded by Hurricane Gilbert in 1988 and again by Wilma, which blasted the resort in 2005. However, scientists believe that people are also to blame for the loss of sand from the barrier. Sand was taken from the beach during the 1970s and 80s to be used in the construction of the hotels. Some hotels built vertical sea walls to protect their property. These divert the energy of the wave downwards and cause scouring of sand from the beach. Scientists fear that these changes have left the resort more vulnerable to coastal erosion and to flooding during tropical storms.

Artificial reefs

In 1998 engineers pumped a mixture of sea water and sand into several fabric tubes known as 'sandtainers'. These tubes were positioned in two lines to make a pair of artificial reefs parallel to the shore. The finished reef was 800 m long. It encouraged the deposition of sediment behind the reef and also on the beach.

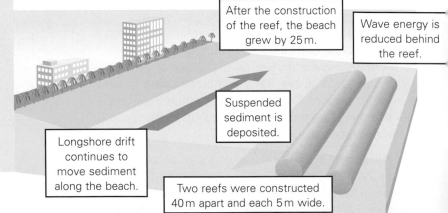

After the construction of the reef, the beach grew by 25 m.

Wave energy is reduced behind the reef.

Suspended sediment is deposited.

Longshore drift continues to move sediment along the beach.

Two reefs were constructed 40 m apart and each 5 m wide.

Figure 26 Map of the Cancun–Nizuc barrier and detail of the artificial reef built in 1998

Activity

1 Describe how the coastline at Cancun has affected the local economy.

2 Make a copy of Figure 26. Mark on it the direction of longshore drift. Use your diagram to explain how this landform was made.

3 Read Figure 27. Use your map of the Cancun–Nizuc barrier to explain how building a breakwater or groyne outside the Gran Caribe Real Hotel would:
   a) improve business for this hotel
   b) affect the hotels further along the beach (state whether it would have affected hotels to the north or south).

4 Use this case study to explain why the local council should decide how the coast is managed rather than individual land owners.

Beach replenishment

On 21 October 2005 Cancun was hit by Hurricane Wilma which caused widespread damage to the resort's hotels and its beaches. It cost $1.5 billion to repair the damage done by Wilma. One of the biggest challenges was to repair the damage to the beach. The storm surge eroded millions of tonnes of sand from Cancun's beach. The original beach had been 20 m wide and covered in fine white sand. The storm waves eroded all of the sand, exposing the rocky wave-cut platform underneath.

The beach was repaired using a technique known as **beach replenishment**. The work was carried out by a Belgian engineering firm, Jan de Nul, which used a boat to dredge sand from the sea bed and pump it back onto the beach. About 2.7 million m³ of sand were sucked up from two offshore sand banks. The new beach was 45 m wide and 12 km long. It took six months to complete the task, which was finished in June 2006. Beach replenishment is an example of soft engineering where natural materials, in this case sand, are used rather than artificial materials such as concrete.

'Beach war' hotels probed over sand theft

Surprised tourists found their little piece of Cancun beach paradise ringed by crime-scene tape on Thursday. Environmental enforcement officers backed by Mexican navy personnel closed off dozens of metres of powder-white coastline in front of a hotel accused of illegally accumulating sand on its beach.

Mexico spent US$19 million to replace Cancun beaches washed away by Hurricane Wilma in 2005. But much of the sand pumped from the sea floor has since washed away, leading some property owners to build breakwaters in a bid to retain sand. The practice often merely shifts sand loss to beaches below the breakwaters.

'Today we made the decision to close this stretch of ill-gotten, illegally accumulated sand,' said Patricio Patron, Mexico's attorney general for environmental protection. 'This hotel was telling its tourists: "Come here, I have sand ... the other hotels don't, because I stole it."'

Patron said five people were detained in a raid for allegedly using pumps to move sand from the sea floor onto the beach in front of the Gran Caribe Real Hotel. The hotel is also suspected of illegally building a breakwater that impeded the natural flow of sand onto other hotels' beaches.

Figure 27 A news report of conflict over management of the beach at Cancun, Mexico, 31 July 2009

Activity

5   Use evidence from pages 8–15 to complete the following table. Make sure you describe and explain each advantage and disadvantage.

Type of management	Examples	Advantages	Disadvantages
Hard engineering	Breakwaters at Jaywick	Homes are protected so ...	
	Groynes at Borth		
	Sea walls at Cancun		
Soft engineering	Beach replenishment		The process has to be repeated in a few years because ...
	Artificial sandtainer reef at Cancun		

How should coastal environments be managed in the future?

Why are sea levels changing and how will these changes affect people?

Why are sea levels changing?

Sea levels are rising. Scientists in Amsterdam in the Netherlands, began taking measurements of sea level in 1700 and similar readings were started in Liverpool in 1768. Readings taken in Europe and the USA over the last 100 years prove that sea levels have risen by around 180 mm (an average of 1.8 mm per year). This rise is largely due to climate change. Higher temperatures mean two things:

- Warm water expands slightly in volume, so as the oceans get warmer they also get slightly higher.
- The ice sheets that cover large parts of Antarctica and Greenland are melting. As the ice melts, water that has been trapped as ice for tens of thousands of years flows into the oceans.

Figure 28 These icebergs have broken away from the huge Vatnajokull ice sheet in Iceland. As they melt their water flows out into the North Atlantic, adding to the amount of water in that ocean

Why are some coastlines more at risk than others?

As well as the general rise in sea levels of 1.8 mm per year, there are local factors that mean that some coastlines are more at risk than others. This is because some coasts are sinking or subsiding. **Subsidence** can be caused by more than one factor.

- River estuaries and deltas sink under their own weight. A river delta, such as that of the Mississippi in the USA, is made of millions of tonnes of loosely compacted sediment and water. As more sediment is deposited, the particles become more compressed and the water is squeezed out. Parts of the city of New Orleans, USA, are subsiding by 28 mm a year.
- In some parts of England the crust has been sinking ever since the ice melted 10,000 years ago at the end of the Ice Age. Northern parts of the UK were covered by thick layers of heavy ice and the crust was pressed down. When the ice melted, the crust in this part of the UK began to rise slowly. At the same time, the southern part of the UK began to sink. This process is called **postglacial rebound**. The subsidence due to rebound is about 2 mm per year in the south-east of England.

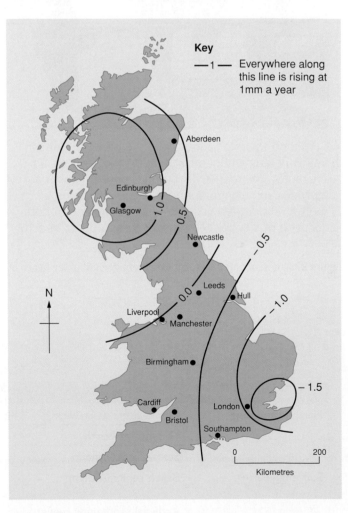

Figure 29 The amount of postglacial rebound (mm per year). Positive numbers mean the land is rising relative to sea level and negative numbers mean the land is sinking

Activity

1 Use Figure 29 to describe the parts of the UK where:
   a) land is rising fastest
   b) land is sinking fastest.

2 Produce a poster or presentation on a computer that explains why sea levels are rising.

Geography Futures

How much will sea level rise in the future?

Predictions of future sea-level rise vary quite a lot. Scientists make their predictions using computer models. They feed data that has already been observed, about such things as carbon dioxide emissions, sea levels and temperatures, into the computer model and the model makes a prediction. The problem is that the processes that take place in our atmosphere, oceans and ice sheets are very complex and it is difficult to model them accurately in a computer program. Some of these different predictions are shown in the purple area of Figure 31. Scientists agree that the complete melting of the Greenland ice sheet would cause a global sea-level rise of between 6 and 7 m. This would probably take many hundreds or thousands of years, although recent evidence suggests that Greenland's ice is melting faster than we originally expected.

Vertical land movement due to postglacial rebound (mm per year)	Sea level rise (mm per year)			
	1990–2025	2025–2055	2055–2085	2085–2115
−0.5	3.5	8.0	11.5	14.5

Figure 30 Predicted change in sea level in south-west England and Wales. Source: Defra

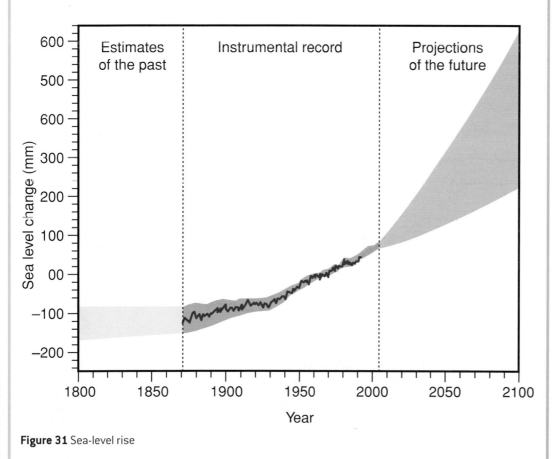

Figure 31 Sea-level rise

Activity

1 **a)** Choose a suitable technique to graph the data in Figure 30.
  b) Calculate the number of years in each of the four time periods. Multiply this by the amount of sea-level rise per year in each period. By how much will average sea level have increased by 2115 in Wales?

2 Study Figure 31.
  a) Describe the shape of the graph between 1870 and 2000.
  b) Use figures from the graph to describe the range of estimates of sea-level rise by 2010.

How will these changes to our coastline affect people?

Rising sea levels will increase the rate of coastal erosion. More farmland will be lost and more expensive sea defences will be needed to 'hold the line' against erosion of our towns and cities. Climate change also means a warmer atmosphere which means more storms like the devastating storm surge that flooded Jaywick in 1953.

In tropical regions the warmer atmosphere will mean more frequent and larger hurricanes flooding coastal regions. The tourist economy of the Caribbean region could be badly affected as beaches are eroded. Small island nations such as the Maldives in the Indian Ocean and the Marshall Islands in the Pacific are very low-lying. A 1 m rise in sea level by 2100 would flood up to 75 per cent of the land of these nations.

The worst-affected coastal communities would be those living on the world's major river deltas. People living here are affected by subsidence of the soft land as well as by sea-level rise. Millions of people live on deltas in Bangladesh, Egypt, Nigeria, Thailand and Cambodia. People will be forced to flee. They would become **environmental refugees**.

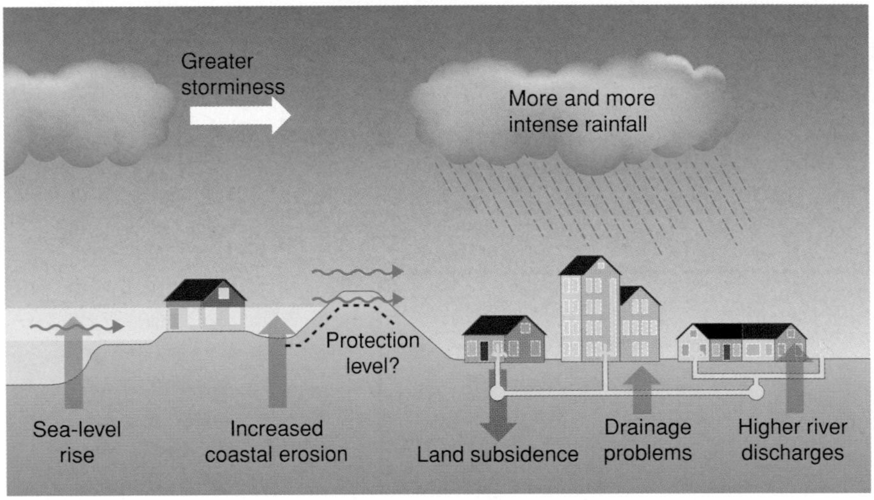

Figure 32 Some of the impacts of climate change on our coastline by 2050

Key
Potential shoreline erosion:
- Low
- Moderate
- High
- Very high
- Extreme

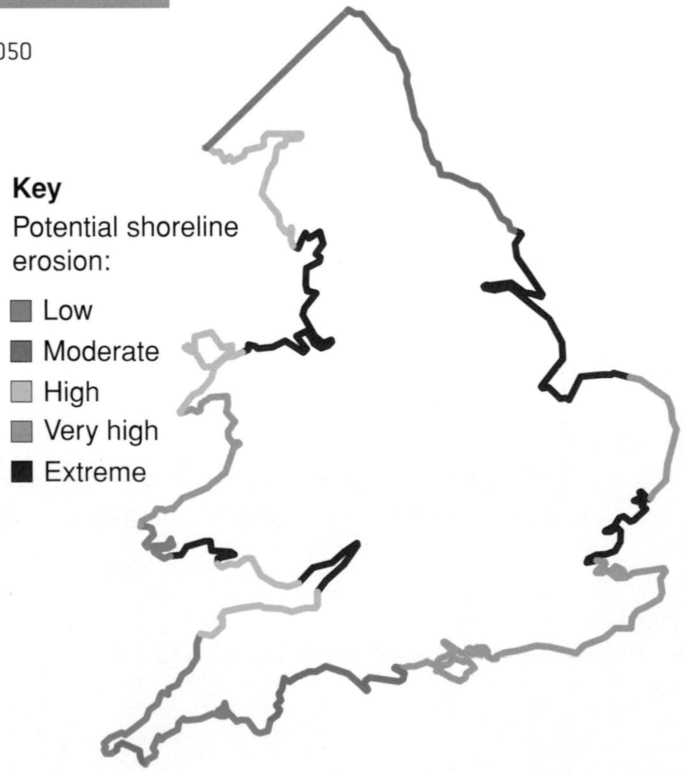

Figure 33 Coastal erosion if carbon dioxide emissions continue to increase and sea levels rise

Geography Futures

What is the most sustainable way to manage our coastline in the face of rising sea levels?

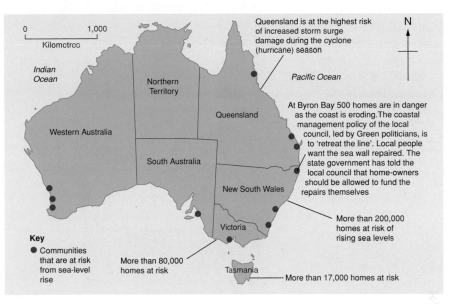

Queensland is at the highest risk of increased storm surge damage during the cyclone (hurricane) season

At Byron Bay 500 homes are in danger as the coast is eroding. The coastal management policy of the local council, led by Green politicians, is to 'retreat the line'. Local people want the sea wall repaired. The state government has told the local council that home-owners should be allowed to fund the repairs themselves

More than 200,000 homes at risk of rising sea levels

More than 80,000 homes at risk

More than 17,000 homes at risk

Key
● Communities that are at risk from sea-level rise

Figure 34 Areas which the Australian government believes are under threat from sea-level rise

Activity

1 Work in pairs and study Figures 34 and 35. On a poster or in a PowerPoint presentation, summarise the main impacts that sea-level rise will have on the Australian coast. Your poster/ presentation should include:
   - graphical techniques to represent the data
   - a summary of the economic impacts and social impacts
   - an explanation of the viewpoints of Byron Bay Council and the opposing view of the residents of Byron Bay.

Climate change threatens Australia's coastal lifestyle, report warns

An Australian government environmental committee report warns that thousands of miles of coastline are under threat from rising sea levels and suggests banning people from living in vulnerable areas.

Beach culture is as much part of the Australian identity as the bush and barbecues, but that could have to change according to a government report that raises the unsettling prospect of banning its citizens from coastal regions at risk of rising seas. The report, from a parliamentary climate change committee, said that AUS$150bn (£84bn) worth of property was at risk from rising sea levels and more frequent storms. With 80 per cent of Australians living along the coastline, the report warns that 'the time to act is now'.

Australia has no national coastal plan despite the prospect of losing large swaths of coastal land as each centimetre rise in sea levels is expected to carve a metre or more off the shoreline. If sea levels rise 80 cm by 2100, some 711,000 homes, businesses and properties, which sit less than 6 m above sea level and lie within 3 km of the coast, will be vulnerable to flooding, erosion, high tides and surging storms. It argues that Australia needs a

national policy to respond to sea level rise brought on by global warming, which could see people forced to abandon homes and banned from building at the beachside, according to the committee on climate change, water, environment and the arts.

Among the report's 47 recommendations are that the government could consider 'forced retreats', and prohibiting the 'continued occupation of the land or future building development on the property due to sea hazard'.

Some members of the conservative Liberal-National party coalition, which voted down the Rudd government's carbon emissions trading scheme earlier this year, remain sceptical that a problem exists. Liberal MP Tony Abbott, a senior member of the coalition and leadership contender, said there was no reason for alarm. 'When it comes to rising sea levels I'm alert but I can't say that I'm particularly alarmed. The fact is that sea levels have risen along the NSW coast by more than 20 cm over the last century. Has anyone noticed it? No they haven't. Obviously an 80 cm rise in sea levels would be more serious but I'm confident that we have the resources to cope,' Abbott told ABC news.

Figure 35 News extract from the *Guardian*, 27 October 2009

Is managed realignment the most sustainable option for the future?

The Essex coastline contains many creeks, salt marshes and mud banks (as you can see in grid square 0913 in Figure 23 on page 12. These features are a natural water store and help to soak up water during a storm surge. However, as sea levels rise, they are rapidly being eroded, as you can see in Figure 37. The erosion of these salt marshes leaves Essex even more vulnerable to coastal floods in the future.

Activity

1 Use Figure 36 to describe the location of Tollesbury.

2 Make a copy of Figure 37.
   a) Calculate the amount of salt marsh that will be left in each estuary by 2050.
   b) Make a simple sketch of Figure 36. Add bars to your map to represent the amount of land eroded in estuary by 2050. Locate your bars in the correct locations.

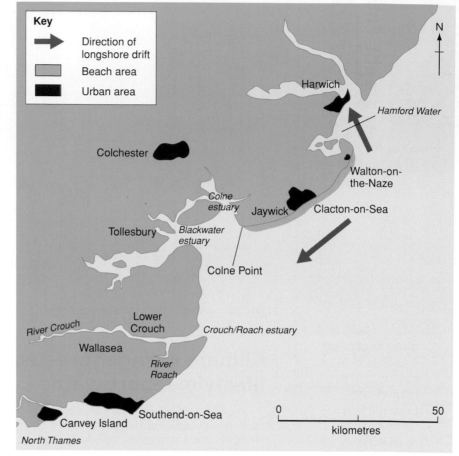

Figure 36 Location of different management techniques on the Essex coast

Estuary	Area in 1998 (hectares)	Area (hectares) eroded by 2050 at present rates	Area (hectares) left by 2050
North Thames	181	−175	
Crouch/Roach	308	−198	
Blackwater	684	−274	
Colne	695	−247	
Hamford Water	621	−722	

Figure 37 Predicted future erosion of salt marsh in Essex estuaries

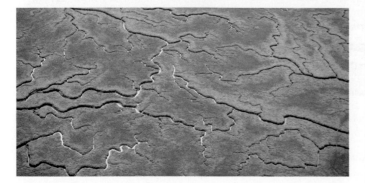

Figure 38 Salt marshes seen from the air

Activity

3 Use Figure 39 to describe:
   a) the distribution of breaches
   b) the amount and value of flooded land.

4 Suggest why the cost of flood damage in Essex would be lower than that in London.

5 Explain how managed realignment in Essex could protect people who live in London in the future.

Figure 39 The cost of flood damage in 2050 after a flood similar to the 1953 storm surge

Legend

	0 €/m²
	0 - 1 €/m²
	1 - 10 €/m²
	10 - 100 €/m²
	100 - 200 €/m²
	200 - 1000 €/m²
	1000 - 2000 €/m²
	2000 - 5000 €/m²
	5000 - 10.000 €/m²
	> 10.000 €/m²
●	Breach location

Managed realignment is being tested near Tollesbury in the Blackwater estuary, and at also at Wallasea in the Crouch estuary. Old earth embankments have kept the sea off these low-lying fields for centuries. Holes have now been punched through the embankments. This is an example of 'retreating the line' which is an option available in all Shoreline Management Plans.

The invading sea water moves slowly across the land at high tide and as it does so it deposits mud. This process recreates natural mudflats and salt marshes. The deposits of mud will absorb wave energy and act as a natural buffer against erosion. The marshes will also help to store water during a storm surge. During a massive flood storm surge, like the one of 1953 that flooded Jaywick, these salt marshes would be flooded. They would store floodwater, meaning that less floodwater would enter the Thames estuary. This should help prevent flooding of many homes and businesses in the Thames estuary and London.

Before

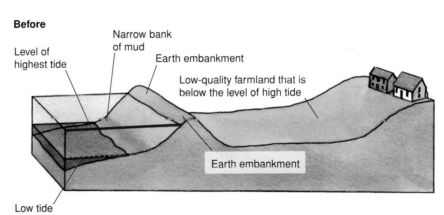

After

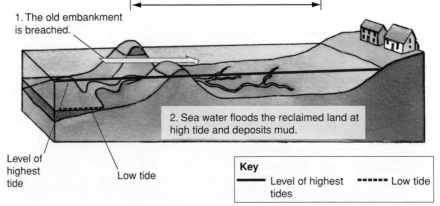

Figure 40 How managed realignment protects the coast

Is everyone in favour of managed realignment?

Managed realignment is much cheaper than hard engineering. Some scientists say it is more sustainable too. Sea walls need constant repair and as sea levels rise will need to be made bigger and stronger. Managed realignment creates a natural buffer zone between coastal communities and the sea. As we have seen, it could even help prevent a disastrous flood in London.

Activity

1 Work in pairs.
   a) Suggest why so many new homes are needed.
   b) List five groups who might oppose plans for new housing and five who might benefit from it.

2 How would you manage the Essex coastline? Produce a report. Include:
   a) a description of the advantages and disadvantages of managed realignment
   b) an explanation of the different points of view about how this coast should be managed
   c) the reason you think that your decision is sustainable.

Figure 41 Opinions about coastal management in Essex

The cost of maintaining the sea defences along many parts of the Essex coast is greater than the benefits of those defences. The land is poor-quality farmland. It doesn't make sense to keep paying for the maintenance of structures like groynes.

The council should be strengthening sea defences all along the Essex coast like they have at Jaywick. My family has lived here and farmed this land for generations. The old embankment has kept the sea out for many years. I don't believe that a rise in sea level of a few centimetres will make any difference.

Farmer

Government (Defra) spokesperson

The UK is experiencing a housing crisis. It is estimated that at least an extra 223,000 new houses or flats are needed every year. That's an extra 3 million homes between 2007 and 2020. The greatest demand for new housing is in the south-east of England. One location where we want to see a lot of new homes is in the Thames Gateway which is on both sides of the Thames estuary. We need a coastal management plan that will protect all of this new housing for at least the next 100 years.

Government housing minister

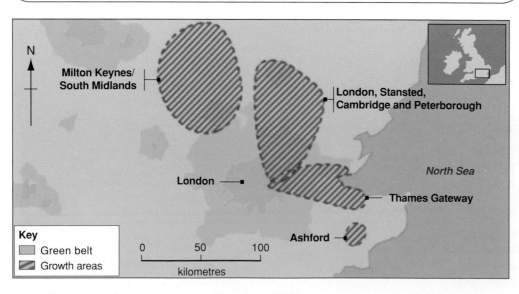

Figure 42 Key areas for new homes in south-east England

What are the differences in climate within the UK?

What's the difference between weather and climate?

One simple answer is that climate is what we expect but weather is what we get!

Weather is our hour-to-hour, day-to-day experience of temperature, cloud cover, precipitation (which includes rain and snow), wind (direction and speed), sunshine and air pressure.

The weather in the UK can be very changeable. The hottest-ever day was recorded in Faversham, Kent, on 10 August 2003. It came during a long period of very hot, dry weather. By comparison, the summer of 2007 was much wetter, causing widespread flooding along the rivers Severn, Thames and Ouse.

The photographs in Figure 1 show examples of the different weather conditions that we experience.

Figure 1 Some of the weather conditions experienced in the UK

Activity

1 What are the elements that make up the weather?

2 Describe fully the weather conditions shown in the photographs in Figure 1.

3 Use www.metoffice.gov.uk to investigate temperature and rainfall records for two contrasting parts of the UK.

Collecting weather data

The weather influences many aspects of our lives. Whether it is wet or dry, hot or cold, it affects many decisions that we take every day:

- What clothes should we wear?
- Will it be safe to travel if it is snowing?
- Will the start of the cricket match be delayed?

We therefore measure aspects of the weather, such as temperature and air pressure, so that we can make forecasts of what the weather will do next. More and more of this data is collected by **remote sensing** equipment, as shown below. On TV and in newspapers the state of the weather at any given time is shown on a weather map, also known as a **synoptic chart**.

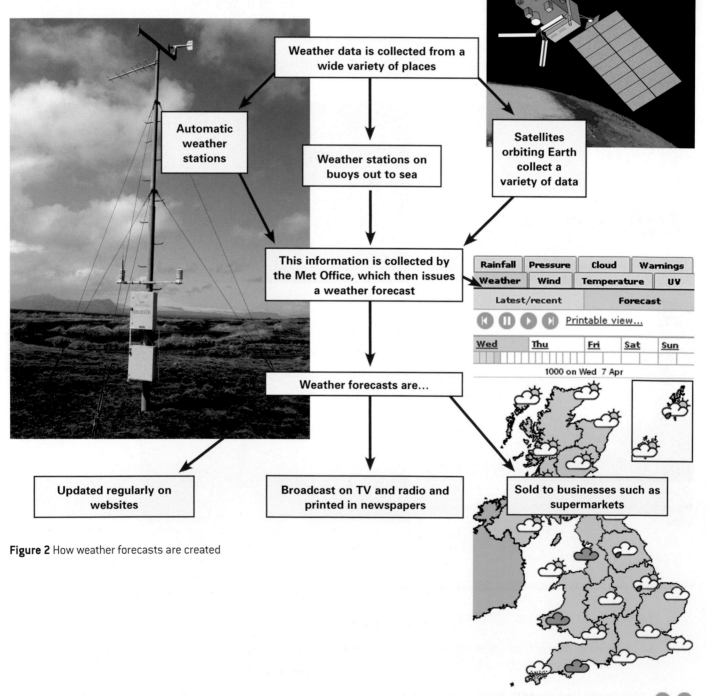

Figure 2 How weather forecasts are created

Updated: 0924 on Wed 7 Apr 2010

Climate is about taking weather readings over long periods of time, and then working out averages, patterns and trends. Different regions of the world have very different and distinctive climates. Iceland, on the edge of the Arctic Circle, has a climate with cold winters and cool summers. By contrast, places along the equator remain hot throughout the year.

Activity

1 Study Figure 3. Write a short weather forecast for a newspaper or prepare a one-minute forecast for a radio programme.

2 Explain how fog might cause problems for:
a) transport
b) leisure activities.

3 Use www.metoffice.gov.uk to study current satellite images and rainfall radar images. Use the images to annotate a simple sketch map of the UK. Label your map with descriptions of the weather in four different places.

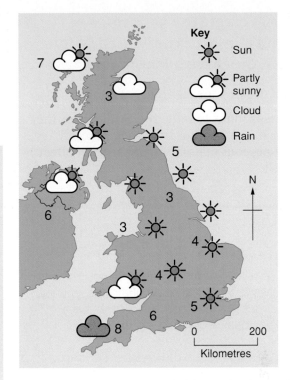

Figure 3 A synoptic chart for the UK forecasting the weather for midday

Describing a climate graph

A climate graph has four features that you need to describe. Study the graph and ask yourself:

1 What is the total annual rainfall? This is calculated by adding all of the values for the rainfall bars together.
2 Are there distinctive wet and dry seasons? If so, when are they, and how long does each last?
3 What is the annual temperature range? This is the difference in temperature between the hottest and coldest times of the year.
4 Does the temperature show a distinctive seasonal pattern? If so, at what time of year are the hot and cold seasons?

• You will get higher marks if you can quantify your answer. This means using significant figures from the graph to add quantities to your description.
• You only need to describe the graph. Don't try to explain the features unless the question has asked you to explain them.

Sample question

Study Figure 4. Describe the main features of the climate of Reykjahlid. [4]

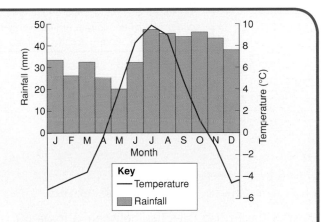

Figure 4 Climate graph for Reykjahlid in northern-central Iceland

Student answer

Reykjahlid has a total annual rainfall of around 430mm.✓ Between December and April because temperatures are so low rain may fall as snow.✓ Rainfall in the summer is slightly higher✓ than in winter. There is a big difference✓ between summer and winter temperatures. The warmest temperatures are in August, about 10° and the lowest in January, about −5 °C✓, a difference of around 15 °C.✓

What the examiner has to say!

This is an excellent description and easily scores the maximum 4 marks.

What factors create the variations in weather and climate experienced within and around the British Isles?

How do air masses affect the weather?

When **air masses** move towards the British Isles they bring with them the weather from their place of origin. There are four main air masses which affect the British Isles.

Activity

1 a) Name the four air masses that affect the British Isles.

b) Use an atlas or a map on the internet. For each air mass suggest the name of a place, country, sea or ocean that the air mass might have come across before reaching the UK.

2 Work in pairs to explain the weather conditions associated with each air mass.

Polar maritime (Pm)
Air from the north or north-west. Gives cool or cold conditions with prolonged periods of rain. A very common air mass.

Polar continental (Pc)
Air from the east or north-east. Gives cold/very cold and dry conditions.

Tropical maritime (Tm)
Air from the west or south-west. Gives mild or warm conditions with prolonged periods of rain. A very common air mass.

Tropical continental (Tc)
Air from the south or south-east. Gives hot and dry conditions.

Figure 5 Air masses which affect the British Isles

How does latitude affect temperature?

Most of the British Isles lies between latitude 50°N and 60°N. This 10° difference in latitude means that the southern parts of the country are usually warmer than the north. Figure 6 shows the difference in average temperatures between Oxford, England and Kirkwall, Scotland. However, this temperature pattern can be distorted as a result of two other factors which affect climate:

- closeness to the sea
- altitude.

Place	Latitude	Max. temp	Min. temp
Oxford	51°N	14·1°C	6·7°C
Kirkwall	59°N	10·5°C	5·3°C

Figure 6 Average temperatures for two UK cities (1971–2000)

Activity

3 Study figure 6.
a) Use an atlas to describe the location of Oxford and Kirkwall.
b) Describe and explain the differences in temperature between the two places.

4 a) Use Figure 8 to calculate the annual temperature range for:
i) Plymouth
ii) Prague.
b) Explain the temperature differences between Plymouth and Prague.
c) Using Figure 8 to help you, suggest how the colder winter temperatures in Prague might affect people, transport and businesses.

How does the sea affect temperatures?

Ocean currents are able to transfer heat from warm latitudes to cooler ones. The west coast of Britain is kept much warmer in winter than other places in similar latitudes by one such current of warm water, the North Atlantic Drift (more commonly known as the Gulf Stream). The sea is also able to retain its heat in winter and cools down very slowly. Places towards the centre of Europe and so further away from the sea have much colder winters. For example, Plymouth and Prague are at the same latitude (50°N), but have very different winter temperatures. The warming affect of the sea can have a big impact on climate. For example, Inverewe Gardens are located to the north of Gairloch on the north-west coast of Scotland at a latitude of 58°N. Even at this high latitude a range of exotic plants such as palm trees can flourish.

Average temperature °C	Plymouth	Prague
January	6	-2·5
July	16	18

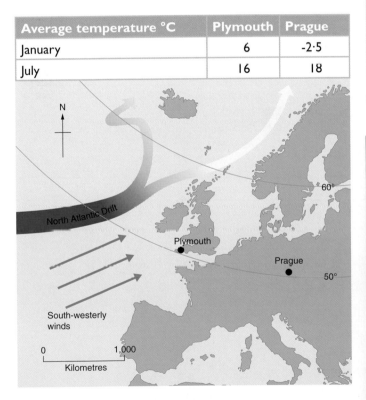

Figure 8 Comparing Plymouth and Prague

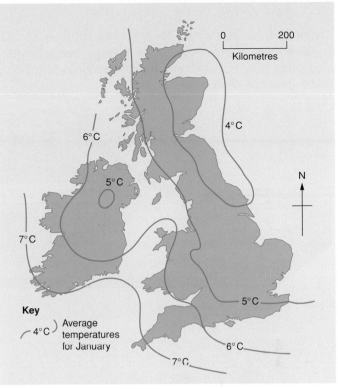

Figure 7 Average temperatures for January

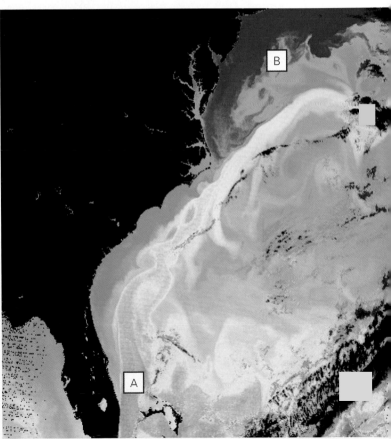

Figure 9 Satellite image of the Gulf Stream. The orange colours show warm water. Cold water is blue. Land is black

Activity

5　**a)** Use Figure 7 to describe the January temperature pattern for the British Isles.

　　b) The lines on the map are called *isotherms*. Suggest a definition for this term.

6　Study Figure 9. Describe what is happening at A and B.

How does altitude affect rainfall?

Britain's prevailing winds are from the south-west. These winds, which blow from the warm sea in winter, also bring moist conditions. **Relief rainfall** is formed as moist onshore winds meet high land.

Figure 10 Cross-section through England and Wales

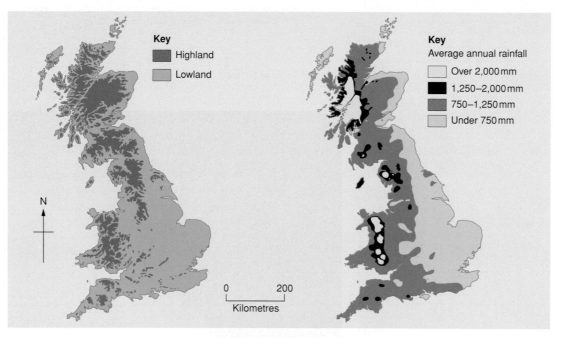

Figure 11 The distribution of upland areas of the UK and average annual rainfall

Activity

1   Make a copy of Figure 10. Position the additional labels below in suitable places on your diagram. Be prepared to explain your decisions.
    - The mountains force the air to rise
    - The rain shadow – an area of low rainfall
    - The wind often blows in from the south-west
    - Cloud and eventually rain is formed
    - The air sinks and warms
    - As the air rises it cools and water vapour condenses

2   Study Figure 11 and an atlas.
    a)   Identify the main mountainous regions of the British Isles. Locate and name them on an outline map.
    b)   Describe and explain the relationship between relief and rainfall shown by the two maps.

How does altitude affect temperature?

The highland areas of the British Isles tend to be much colder than the lowlands. Temperatures decrease by 1 °C for every 100 m in height. This is because **solar radiation** (heat from the sun) passes directly through the atmosphere, heating the Earth's surface. Warm air rises from the Earth's surface as convection currents. As the air rises it then cools.

Snowdonia

<u>Wednesday</u>

Weather

Cloudy with occasional outbreaks of rain or drizzle during the morning. Some drier, brighter spells are likely to the lee of high ground. During the afternoon rain and drizzle will turn more persistent and heavier later.

Visibility

The visibility will be good at lower levels, but moderate in rain and poor in hill fog.

Hill fog

Hill fog will be patchy with cloud bases around 600 to 700 metres during the morning. Cloud bases will lower to 300 to 400 metres in the west later as rain becomes heavier.

Maximum winds above 500 metres

Strong to gale southerly winds with speeds 30 to 40 mph will gust to 50 or 60 mph at times over exposed peaks and ridges.

Temperature

Valleys	Plus 20 degrees Celsius
900 metres	Plus 12 degrees Celsius
Freezing level	Will be above the peaks.

Source: Met Office

Figure 12 Weather forecast for Snowdonia, 19 August 2009

Activity

3 **a)** Use Figure 12 to describe how altitude affects the weather in Snowdonia.

b) Suggest how a walker visiting the mountain should prepare for their walk.

4 The highest mountain in Britain is Ben Nevis at 1,344 m. What should the temperature difference be between the summit and sea level?

Figure 13 The summit of Snowdon in winter

Aspect – a local influence on climate?

Aspect is the direction a place or slope faces. The influence of aspect can be clearly seen in a case study of the Vale of Llangollen in north-east Wales. Slope A on the Ordnance Survey extract (Figure 15) is north facing which means it has a northerly aspect. Slope B, on the other hand, has a southerly aspect. In winter slopes which face south are warmer than those that face north. This is because in winter the sun is low in the sky and shines on the south facing slope only. The side facing north is in shadow and this has the effect of lowering temperatures.

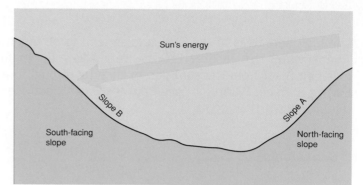

Figure 14 Why is aspect a factor in controlling winter temperatures?

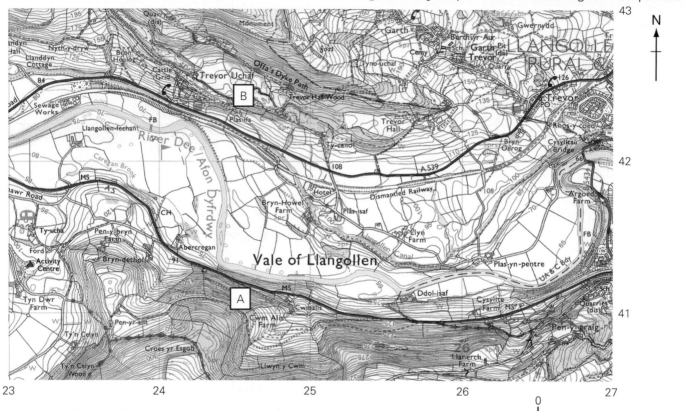

Figure 15 An Ordnance Survey extract of the Vale of Llangollen. Scale 1:25,000 Sheet 256

Figure 16 View towards slope A – the north-facing slope

Activity

1. How does the OS map in Figure 15 indicate that slope A (Figure 16) is very steep?

2. Use Figure 14 to explain why slope A has lower temperatures in winter.

3. There are a number of woodland areas on the map in Figure 15.
   a) Give a grid reference for a woodland on a north-facing slope.
   b) Suggest and plan an enquiry that you could undertake to show that woodlands have their own climate.

How does the weather create hazards for people?

What type of weather is associated with low and high pressure?

The latitude of the British Isles is within a belt that gets a mixture of high and low pressure. These pressure systems bring with them very different patterns of weather.

High pressure

Areas of high pressure are also known as **anticyclones**. Anticyclones bring dry, settled periods of weather. Winds are usually light (or non-existent) and blow in a clockwise direction. In summer a lack of cloud gives very warm, sunny conditions. If an anticyclone becomes fixed over the British Isles in winter the weather is sunny and dry but cold, and especially cold at night. As a result frost and fog are quite common.

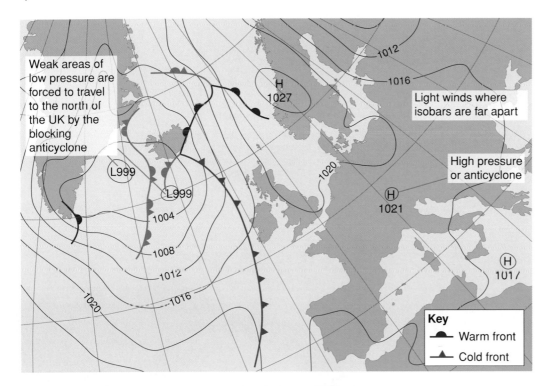

Weak areas of low pressure are forced to travel to the north of the UK by the blocking anticyclone

Light winds where isobars are far apart

High pressure or anticyclone

Key
— Warm front
— Cold front

Figure 17 A weather map showing an anticyclone in August 2003

Activity

4 a) Use an atlas to describe the location of each of the areas of high pressure shown in Figure 17.

b) The weather in France in August 2003 was record-breaking. Use the internet to research the weather conditions at this time.

5 Explain how clear skies and calm conditions can allow frost and fog to form.

Low pressure

Regions of low pressure in the atmosphere are formed when air lifts off the Earth's surface. It is common for several cells of low pressure, also known as **depressions**, to form in the North Atlantic at any one time. They then track eastwards towards the British Isles bringing changeable weather characterised by wind, cloud and rain. Inside the depression there is a battle between huge masses of warmer and colder air. These air masses revolve slowly around each other in an anti-clockwise direction. As the lighter, warmer air rises and cools, its moisture condenses, forming huge banks of cloud. Seen from above, these curving banks of cloud give the depression a characteristic shape (Figure 19).

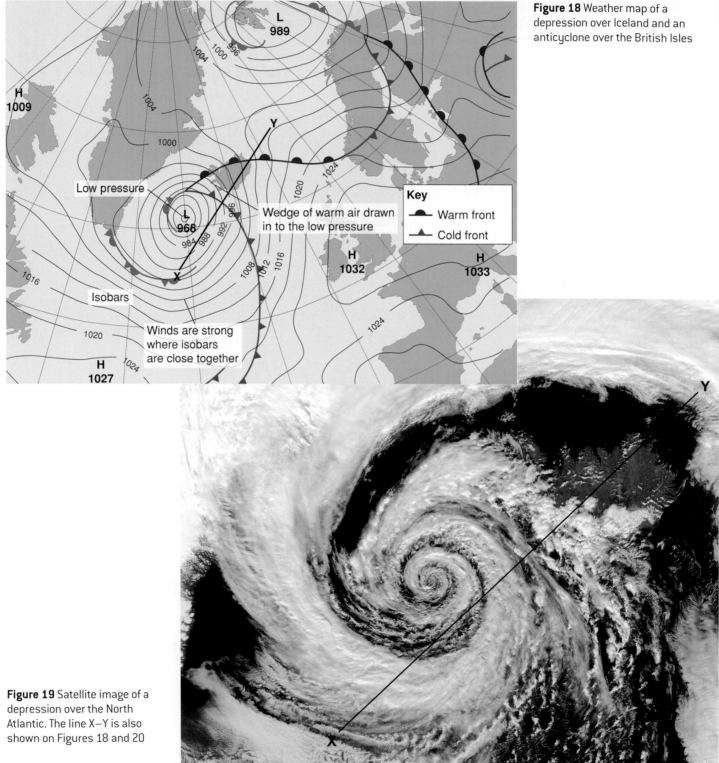

Figure 18 Weather map of a depression over Iceland and an anticyclone over the British Isles

Figure 19 Satellite image of a depression over the North Atlantic. The line X–Y is also shown on Figures 18 and 20

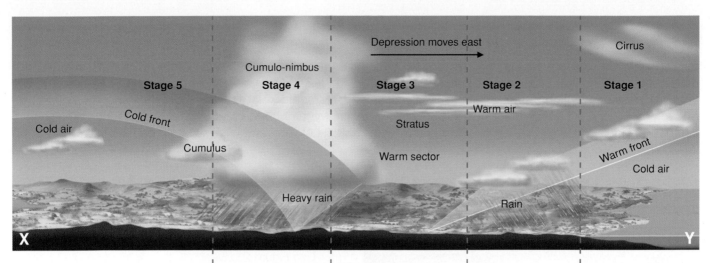

	Stage 5	Stage 4	Stage 3	Stage 2	Stage 1
Air mass	Cold	Cold			
Temperature °C		7	11	6	5
Wind strength		Very strong	Strong		
Wind direction	SSW	S	SSE	SE	E
Cloud/rain		Thick, low cloud and heavy rain	Some high cloud and clear skies. No rain		

Figure 20 Weather associated with the easterly progress of the depression shown in Figure 19

Feature	Cyclones or depressions	Anticyclones
Air pressure		High, usually above 1020 mb (millibars)
Air movement	Rising	
Wind strength	Strong	
Wind circulation		Clockwise
Typical winter weather		Cold and dry. Clear skies in the daytime. Frost at night.
Typical summer weather	Mild and wet. Cloudy with periods of heavy rain separated by showers.	

Figure 21 Comparing depressions and anticyclones

Activity

1 a) Use Figure 20 to explain how rain is formed at a warm front.
   b) Draw your own diagram to show how rain is formed at a cold front.

2 a) Make a copy of the table in Figure 20. Use the evidence in Figures 18, 19 and 20 to complete the missing sections.
   b) Imagine you are a weather forecaster working in north-west Iceland. Prepare a local weather forecast for the next few hours.

3 Make a large copy of Figure 21 and use the information on pages 31–3 to complete the blank spaces.

What are the weather hazards associated with high and low pressure systems?

During the summer of 2007 the jet stream was much further south than usual, bringing a series of slow-moving depressions that caused record-breaking rainfall on 13–15 June and again on 24–25 June. Even more rain fell on 19 and 20 July. In fact, many parts of central England had over 100 mm of rainfall on 20 July: that's more than the usual amount for the whole month. By now the ground was saturated with water and no more could soak in. Rivers burst their banks and the UK suffered its worst floods in living memory. As well as heavy rain, low pressure systems can bring damaging gusts of wind and large waves onto the coast.

Figure 22 Flooding at Tewkesbury on the confluence of the rivers Severn and Avon

Activity

1 Use pages 31–34 to name all the weather hazards associated with low and high pressure.

2 Use Figure 23. Describe the distribution of places that had:
   a) less than 70 per cent of normal rainfall
   b) more than 85 per cent of normal rainfall.

3 Suggest how both a flood and a drought might affect:
   a) a pensioner living alone
   b) a small business, for example a shopkeeper
   c) a cattle or arable farmer.

4 Research why parts of eastern England are particularly prone to coastal flooding.

In the summer of 2006, parts of England were suffering their worst **drought** for 30 years. The water shortage was worst in south-east England. By February 2006 this region had experienced fourteen consecutive months of below-average rainfall as a result of persistent anticyclonic conditions. Then June and July were unusually hot.

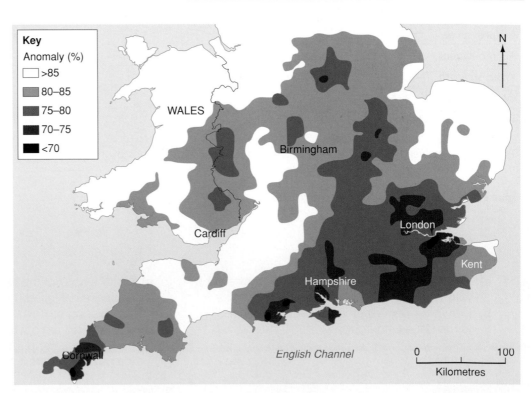

Figure 23 Distribution of rainfall anomaly (percentage of average rainfall totals) in Wales and Southern England

Burma   What are the weather hazards associated with tropical storms?

Severe storms that occur in tropical regions (known as hurricanes, cyclones or typhoons) are caused by very low air pressure. They get their energy from the warm tropical seas beneath them. The sea has to be at a temperature of at least 26 °C for a few weeks to generate such a storm. The warm water acts like fuel. It heats the air above it, which rises, creating storm clouds and heavy rainfall. The storm loses strength when it moves over land and loses its fuel supply.

In early May 2008, Cyclone Nargis crossed the Bay of Bengal and hit the coast of Burma (Myanmar). The very low air pressure meant that there was less pressure on the surface of the ocean from above. Consequently the ocean bulged upwards beneath the storm, creating a **storm surge**, and sea level rose by 3.6 m. Unfortunately the storm hit the coast at high tide, meaning that the storm surge was higher than the level of the flat coastal plain. As the storm tracked along the densely populated southern coastline of Burma, the storm surge caused flooding for long distances inland. In addition to this the strong storm winds, which peaked at 215 km/hr, blowing over the ocean created huge waves. It is thought these waves reached a maximum height of 7.6 m above the level of the storm surge.

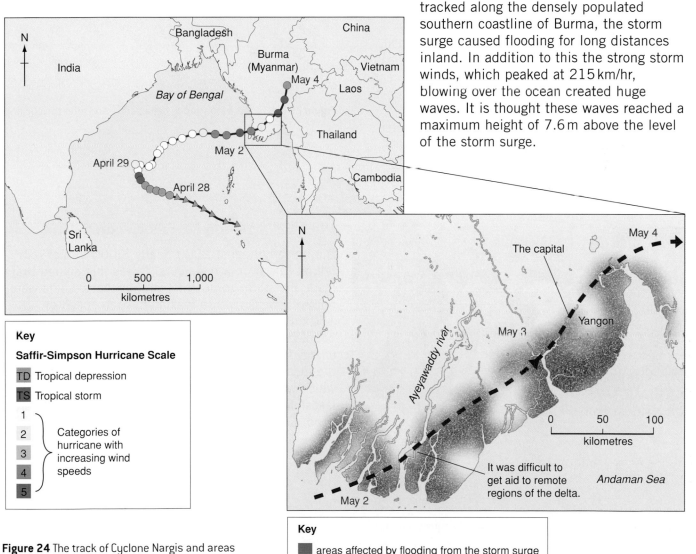

Key

Saffir-Simpson Hurricane Scale

TD Tropical depression

TS Tropical storm

1
2 } Categories of
3   hurricane with
4   increasing wind
       speeds
5

Figure 24 The track of Cyclone Nargis and areas affected by flooding

Key

■ areas affected by flooding from the storm surge

Activity

5 Outline the cause of the severe weather that affected Burma in May 2008.

6 a) Describe the track of Cyclone Nargis.
   b) Describe the distribution of land affected by flooding.

7 Research hurricanes/cyclones further. Focus on:
   • which parts of the tropics are affected by hurricanes
   • a case study of a recent hurricane
   • the Saffir-Simpson Hurricane Scale.

How do weather hazards affect people, the economy and the environment?

How were people affected by Cyclone Nargis?

Nargis and its terrible floodwaters affected people in both the short term and the long term. About 800,000 homes were damaged and many survivors were displaced. Most of these moved in with family members and 260,000 moved into refugee camps. Surprisingly, 80 per cent of the damaged homes were rebuilt by the end of June 2008. Land was flooded and rice crops destroyed. Over half of the survivors (an estimated 130,000 people were killed, most by drowning) in the worst-hit areas were short of food. Around 65 per cent of the population reported health problems in early June. These included 37 per cent of the population suffering from fever and 34 per cent from diarrhoea. Diseases such as diarrhoea are common after such events, because drinking water becomes polluted with sewage. Three-quarters of health centres in the region were damaged by the storm, so families had less access to immunisation and other types of care when they needed it most.

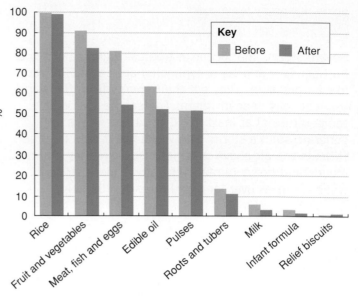

Figure 25 Diet in the Ayeyawaddy delta before and after the cyclone

Figure 26 Villagers are rescued from floods in Cangnan county, eastern China

Why was Typhoon Morakot so destructive?

During early August 2009 nearly 3,000 mm of rain fell on Taiwan in a few hours. It was this deluge that made the storm so destructive. Morakot's winds were relatively weak, with a maximum wind speed of 150 km/hr. However, on 7 August the typhoon doubled in diameter to 1,600 km as it picked up energy from the 28 °C Pacific waters. Worst-hit was the mountain village of Hsiaolin in southern Taiwan which was almost totally destroyed by a massive **landslide**. More than 700 people were missing, feared dead. Eastern China was also badly hit by the storm.

Activity

1 Study Figure 25. Compare the quality of the diet before and after Cyclone Nargis and suggest how this may have affected the people.

2 Draw a map to show the location of Taiwan and other countries in the region.

3 a) Explain why Typhoon Morakot was so destructive.

   b) Suggest why some areas of this relatively wealthy Asian country were more badly affected than others.

How do weather hazards affect the economy of Iceland?

Iceland's climate has always been a challenge to the Icelandic people. Snow in winter closes many roads and some are not passable until May. Figure 27 summarises some of the impacts of Iceland's climate on the country's economy and its people.

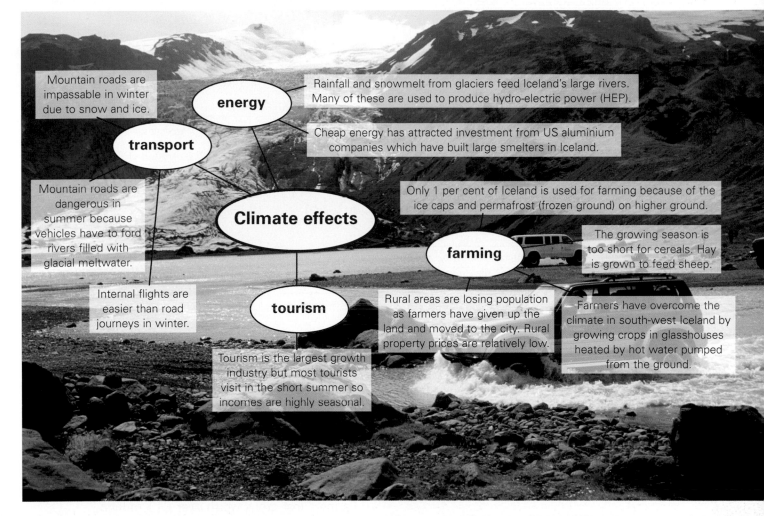

Mountain roads are impassable in winter due to snow and ice.

energy

Rainfall and snowmelt from glaciers feed Iceland's large rivers. Many of these are used to produce hydro-electric power (HEP).

transport

Cheap energy has attracted investment from US aluminium companies which have built large smelters in Iceland.

Mountain roads are dangerous in summer because vehicles have to ford rivers filled with glacial meltwater.

Climate effects

Only 1 per cent of Iceland is used for farming because of the ice caps and permafrost (frozen ground) on higher ground.

farming

The growing season is too short for cereals. Hay is grown to feed sheep.

Internal flights are easier than road journeys in winter.

tourism

Rural areas are losing population as farmers have given up the land and moved to the city. Rural property prices are relatively low.

Farmers have overcome the climate in south-west Iceland by growing crops in glasshouses heated by hot water pumped from the ground.

Tourism is the largest growth industry but most tourists visit in the short summer so incomes are highly seasonal.

Figure 27 How Iceland's climate affects the economy

Is the UK economy ever affected?

Between 20 and 22 December 2006 an area of high pressure settled over the UK. This trapped and prevented cool air from rising. Moisture in the air condensed, forming thick fog. Several airlines had to cancel flights and compensate their passengers or find them alternative transport arrangements by train or coach. For example, on 22 December a total of 411 flights were cancelled from UK airports, including 350 from Heathrow. At least 40,000 people were affected by the travel chaos: this should have been the busiest day of the Christmas holiday.

Activity

4 a) Use Figure 27 to explain how Iceland's climate affects its people.

   b) Use the website of the Icelandic Met Office to research the effects of extreme weather, including avalanches. Follow this link:

   http://en.vedur.is/avalanches/articles

5 What are the economic effects of tropical storms? Use specific examples from different parts of the world in your investigation.

How do hazards create short-term and long-term effects?

In June, July and August 2007 the UK suffered its worst floods in living memory. Heavy rainfall in June caused flooding in the East Midlands and Yorkshire. More heavy rain in July caused flooding along the rivers Severn, Thames and Ouse. The floods caused loss of life, widespread damage to property and disruption to transport.

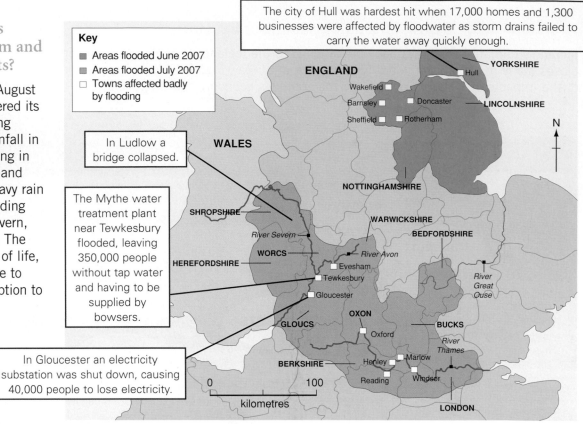

The city of Hull was hardest hit when 17,000 homes and 1,300 businesses were affected by floodwater as storm drains failed to carry the water away quickly enough.

Key
- ■ Areas flooded June 2007
- ■ Areas flooded July 2007
- □ Towns affected badly by flooding

In Ludlow a bridge collapsed.

The Mythe water treatment plant near Tewkesbury flooded, leaving 350,000 people without tap water and having to be supplied by bowsers.

In Gloucester an electricity substation was shut down, causing 40,000 people to lose electricity.

Figure 28 The areas affected by the summer floods of 2007

Thousands of motorists were stranded as roads became impassable and motorways closed. As many as 10,000 people were stranded on the M5 motorway. Rivers overflowed their banks, destroying crops that were ready for harvesting. In towns and cities the sewage and drainage systems could not cope with the huge quantities of water causing flooding of streets, homes and businesses.

The disaster continued to affect people and businesses even after the floodwaters had gone down. Many people whose homes had been flooded had to stay with relatives or in caravans and hotels. Businesses had to be cleared out and many lost orders whilst they repaired the damage. Some children had to be taught in temporary classrooms without books, which had been lost in the floods. Farmers lost crops worth over £11 million.

Figure 29 The impact of the floods in Catcliffe

Activity

1 Use Figure 28 to compare the distribution of the areas affected by the floods in June and July 2007.

2 Use evidence in the photograph (Figure 29) to suggest how quality of life was affected by the flooding.

3 In small groups discuss the difference between short-term and long-term effects, using examples from these pages.

Australia — How do weather hazards affect the environment?

Starting at the end of January 2009, south-east Australia had days of very hot weather, called a **heatwave**. By February the temperature in Victoria reached 47 °C and wind speed was more than 100 km/hr. A ten-year drought had also made the land and forests very dry (many species of trees and shrubs that are native to Australia contain flammable oil and resins). This combination triggered more than 400 bush fires in the eucalypt forests in Victoria.

Another part of the world that has suffered recently from drought and forest fires is Greece. The impacts were particularly severe during the summer of 2007 and again in August 2009.

Activity

4 Use Figure 30 to outline the main impacts of the forest fires. Use the following headings to organise your notes:
   - environmental
   - economic
   - social

5 Use news sites on the internet to investigate other effects of ten years of drought in south-east Australia.

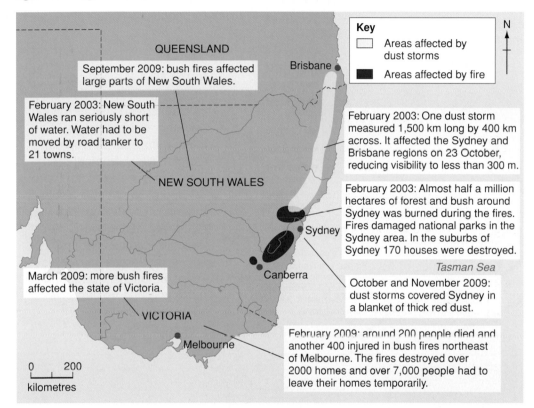

Key
- ☐ Areas affected by dust storms
- ■ Areas affected by fire

N

QUEENSLAND

Brisbane

September 2009: bush fires affected large parts of New South Wales.

February 2003: New South Wales ran seriously short of water. Water had to be moved by road tanker to 21 towns.

February 2003: One dust storm measured 1,500 km long by 400 km across. It affected the Sydney and Brisbane regions on 23 October, reducing visibility to less than 300 m.

NEW SOUTH WALES

February 2003: Almost half a million hectares of forest and bush around Sydney was burned during the fires. Fires damaged national parks in the Sydney area. In the suburbs of Sydney 170 houses were destroyed.

Sydney

Tasman Sea

Canberra

March 2009: more bush fires affected the state of Victoria.

October and November 2009: dust storms covered Sydney in a blanket of thick red dust.

VICTORIA

Melbourne

February 2009: around 200 people died and another 400 injured in bush fires northeast of Melbourne. The fires destroyed over 2000 homes and over 7,000 people had to leave their homes temporarily.

0   200
kilometres

Figure 30 South-east Australia

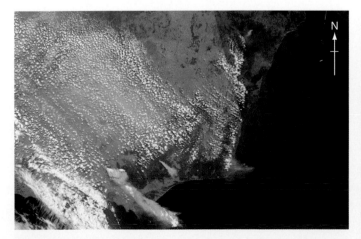

Figure 31 A satellite image of the fires in eastern Victoria, 7 February 2009

Figure 32 Fire rages near homes in the village of Kaletzi, north of Athens

Can we manage weather hazards?

How can technology be used to forecast extreme weather and reduce the impact of its effects?

The European Space Agency provides data to weather forecasters from a combination of two types of satellite:

MeteoStat is a geostationary system in orbit 36,000 km above the Earth. It keeps pace with the Earth's rotation, so it is always above the same point and able to take images of Europe and the Atlantic. This is important because most of the high and low pressure systems that affect Europe come from the Atlantic.

MetOp is a new series of satellites first launched in 2006. This system is in a polar orbit 800 km above the Earth. This means it takes much more detailed readings, and of the whole Earth's surface. This allows scientists to make more accurate medium- and long-term weather forecasts. This should give people more warning of extreme weather events and help to reduce the risk to people from weather hazards.

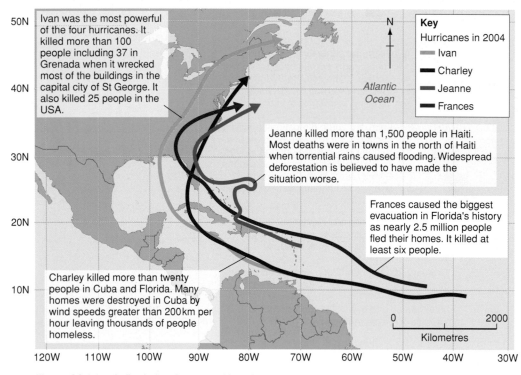

Ivan was the most powerful of the four hurricanes. It killed more than 100 people including 37 in Grenada when it wrecked most of the buildings in the capital city of St George. It also killed 25 people in the USA.

Jeanne killed more than 1,500 people in Haiti. Most deaths were in towns in the north of Haiti when torrential rains caused flooding. Widespread deforestation is believed to have made the situation worse.

Frances caused the biggest evacuation in Florida's history as nearly 2.5 million people fled their homes. It killed at least six people.

Charley killed more than twenty people in Cuba and Florida. Many homes were destroyed in Cuba by wind speeds greater than 200km per hour leaving thousands of people homeless.

Key
Hurricanes in 2004
— Ivan
— Charley
— Jeanne
— Frances

Atlantic Ocean

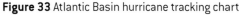

Figure 33 Atlantic Basin hurricane tracking chart

In the USA the National Hurricane Center (NHC), Florida is responsible for tracking and predicting the likely behaviour of tropical storms. When tropical storm conditions are expected within 36 hours, the centre issues the appropriate warnings via the news media and NOAA Weather Radio. The NHC not only gives forecasts but also keeps detailed information on hurricane history and gives advice on hurricane preparedness.

Activity

1 Use the information in Figure 33 to describe the general track taken by these hurricanes.

2 Consider each of the following factors. Explain how it might influence the size of the death toll during a hurricane:
   - wind speed
   - intensity of rainfall
   - population density close to the coast
   - poverty or wealth of the area
   - deforestation.

3 Use **www.esa.int/esaCP/index.html** and follow the multimedia gallery link to find video and animations of the MetOp programme.

4 Use **www.nhc.noaa.gov** to find information on past and current tropical storm events.

Barcelona — Managing drought in Barcelona

Barcelona is the capital city of Catalonia, a prosperous region of north-east Spain. A severe water shortage in 2007/08 forced the city to take extraordinary steps to avoid running out of water. In February 2008 a drought order was imposed. This restricted the use of water by households, for example for watering the garden or washing the car. Water use was restricted in public places such as city parks and 10 per cent of public fountains were turned off. People who broke the rules faced fines. By May 2008 the city was so desperate that a fleet of tankers, each carrying 28 million litres of water, started to bring water into the city's port. This so-called 'water bridge' transferred water to Barcelona from Tarragona in Spain and Marseille in France.

The Catalonian government has suggested that its long-term water supply problem could be solved if water could be transferred into the city from other regions. They have suggested two plans, shown in Figure 34. However, water is a precious resource and both plans have been vigorously opposed. The River Segre runs for part of its course along the border with Aragon and the regional government objects to the use of what it regards as its water in Catalonia. Meanwhile Catalonia has accused Aragon of wanting to use Barcelona's drinking water in the hotels and golf courses of Aragon. Aragon has appealed to the national government. For the moment the national government has backed Aragon and Catalonia cannot go ahead with the plan.

In the meantime Barcelona is counting on a new desalination plant to turn sea water into fresh water. It opened in July 2009.

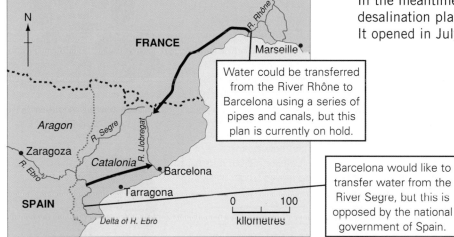

Water could be transferred from the River Rhône to Barcelona using a series of pipes and canals, but this plan is currently on hold.

Barcelona would like to transfer water from the River Segre, but this is opposed by the national government of Spain.

Figure 34 Barcelona's water supply plans

Activity

5 a) List all the solutions to Barcelona's water shortage.

   b) Sort the solutions into things householders could do and things the government did.

   c) What do you think is the most sustainable solution to Barcelona's problem? Justify your answer.

6 Is Aragon right to oppose Catalonia's plan? Write a report stating your point of view.

I belong to a protest group that opposes the plan to transfer water from France. The scheme would damage the ecosystem of the River Rhône. The people who stand to benefit most are the fat cats who own the water companies!

Protestor in France

I'm fed up with the water restrictions. I think our problem is that 70 per cent of Catalonia's water is used by farmers. A lot of them have really old irrigation systems that are leaking and they grow crops that aren't really suited to our dry climate. It's such a waste.

Householder

Building desalination plants is a big mistake. They use huge amounts of energy and therefore contribute to climate change. By building desalination plants Catalonia will actually be increasing the chance of drought. It's just not a sustainable option.

Climate expert

Figure 35 Points of view on the water shortage

| Australia | Reducing the risk of future forest fires |

The forest fires of 2003–9 have encouraged a debate about the management of Australia's forests. Managing the eucalypt forests by controlled burning is one possible way to reduce the risk of fire. Controlled fires clear away the fallen branches and scrub vegetation. This technique reduces the risk of big fires breaking out and spreading out of control. However, the different groups who use the eucalypt forests have different points of view about this issue.

Tourism is an essential part of the New South Wales economy. Tourists want to visit natural, undisturbed, unburned forests. They don't want to see smoke or evidence of fire damage. They also want access to all our forests. Controlled fires would restrict access for tourists.

Hotel owner

We are proud of our culture and tradition of 'firestick' farming (controlled fires). These small fires clear away areas of scrub and encourage the growth of grasses. This management creates a range of habitats ideal for different native animals such as kangaroos.

Controlled burning causes smoke pollution. Smoke is a terrible nuisance and a health hazard. If they are going to manage the forests by burning them, then they can only do it when the weather conditions are just right. It can only be done when the ground is wet, or the fire could spread. Also, there must be no wind or the smoke blows into the suburbs.

Home owner in suburbs of Sydney

Aboriginal representative

Privately owned forests are run as a business. They should be cleared of all shrubs and leaf litter. This reduces the risk of uncontrolled forest fires. It also makes it easier for our cattle to graze in the forest, and allows logging lorries to get in and out of the forest easily.

We are not opposed to the use of controlled burning to reduce shrubs and leaf litter. However, we believe that our national parks should be wild places and that these management techniques should be avoided wherever possible. I don't think that the national parks can be blamed for the fires. Most of the 2003 fires started in privately owned forests and spread into the national parks, not the other way around!

National Park ranger

Private landowner of a forest

Figure 36 Opinions about managing the eucalypt forests

Activity

1 Use the opinions in Figure 36. Copy and complete the following table.

	Arguments for controlled burning	Arguments against controlled burning
Economic		Burning is hazardous and expensive
Environmental		
Social (how different groups might be affected)		Smoke pollution will cause health problems for residents in the suburbs

2 In groups discuss the other possible options that could be used in south-east Australia.

Bangladesh

Can LEDCs manage weather hazards?

Bangladesh is one of the most flood-prone countries in the world. It is affected by river floods and floods due to cyclonic storm surges. In most parts of the country flood control measures are limited to the building of earth embankments which can easily be breached and can be damaged by river **erosion**. However, in the rapidly growing urban areas rivers are being straightened and the banks concreted. Dams are also being constructed upstream. In addition, the Flood Forecasting and Warning System now covers all the flood-prone areas of the country and provides flood information and early warnings.

Similarly the Bangladesh Meteorological Department gives cyclone warnings. As a result many people are evacuated to the cyclone shelters in the coastal region. Unfortunately there is a shortage of shelters and many of those that were built after the 1987 cyclones have worn out and require either major repairs or reconstruction. Sea walls have to be cost effective. One suggestion is to have sea walls with concrete or brick lining on both sides, with the hollow in the middle filled up by sand bags or just sand.

Sundarbans forest has saved many lives and prevented the destruction of property along the coast because it creates a natural barrier against the battering winds of tropical storms. However, this **mangrove** forest could disappear as a result of deforestation.

Figure 37 The location of Bangladesh

Figure 38 Sundarbans forest along the coast of Bangladesh

Activity

3 Use an atlas to discover why the relief of Bangladesh makes it so prone to river flooding.

4 Investigate how human factors also contribute to river flooding.

5 In groups discuss the view that Bangladesh is struggling to cope with hazards.

6 Use pages 14–19 of *GCSE Geography for WJEC A Core* to study how the UK manages the problem of flooding.

Are high-technology strategies always needed?

Rainfall in the **Sahel** region of north Africa is low and extremely variable from year to year. As a result periods of drought are very common. One strategy that has been used successfully in crop-growing regions of Burkina Faso and Mali is the construction of low stone lines known as bunds. Stones are placed along the contours on gentle slopes. Sometimes the bunds are reinforced by planting tough grasses along the lines. The stones and grass encourage rainwater to infiltrate the soil and reduce the amount of rainwater that is lost by run-off. They also prevent soil erosion. In the Sahel soils dry out and are easily eroded by the wind. Farmers report that this technique increases their yields of grain crops. Fields that have stone lines produce 30 per cent more grain than an ordinary field in a year that has poor rainfall, and 20 per cent more in a year that has average rainfall.

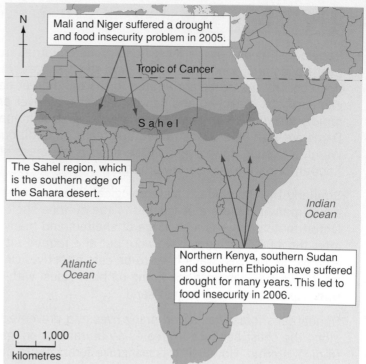

Mali and Niger suffered a drought and food insecurity problem in 2005.

Tropic of Cancer

Sahel

The Sahel region, which is the southern edge of the Sahara desert.

Indian Ocean

Atlantic Ocean

Northern Kenya, southern Sudan and southern Ethiopia have suffered drought for many years. This led to food insecurity in 2006.

0   1,000
kilometres

Figure 39 The location of the Sahel region

Activity

1 Explain how stone lines are able to:
   a) reduce soil erosion
   b) increase soil moisture
   c) increase the amount of grain grown.

2 Tree-planting schemes are also important in the Sahel. Explain how this strategy can help to prevent soil erosion.

3 Investigate the strategies that your local water company has in place to combat a water drought.

4 Working in pairs, discuss all the possible ways that households can save water.

Run-off is slowed by the bund, giving more time for infiltration.

Rainwater infiltrates and recharges soil moisture.

Bunds are placed 10 to 25 m apart.

Any soil that has been eroded by run-off is trapped by the bund. Topsoil and organic matter (e.g. leaf litter) is deposited here.

Figure 40 How bunds work

What are biomes and how do they differ?

What are ecosystems?

An **ecosystem** is community of plants and animals and the environment in which they live. Ecosystems contain both living and non-living parts. The living part includes such things as plants, insects and birds which depend on each other for food. Plants may also depend on insects and birds for pollination and seed dispersal. The non-living part of an ecosystem includes such things as the climate, soils and rocks. This non-living environment provides nutrients, warmth, water and shelter for the living parts of the ecosystem.

Activity

1 Use Figure 1.
   a) Describe three non-living parts of the **tundra** ecosystem.
   b) Describe two ways that nutrients enter into the soil.
   c) Draw a food chain that includes meadow pipit.
   d) What would happen to the merlin if the population of meadow pipits fell for some reason (perhaps because a new predator was introduced to Iceland)?

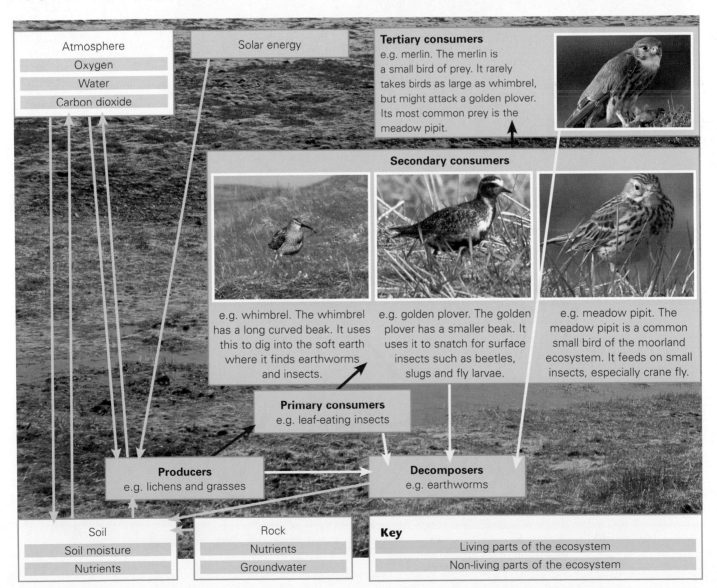

Tertiary consumers
e.g. merlin. The merlin is a small bird of prey. It rarely takes birds as large as whimbrel, but might attack a golden plover. Its most common prey is the meadow pipit.

Secondary consumers

Atmosphere
Oxygen
Water
Carbon dioxide

Solar energy

e.g. whimbrel. The whimbrel has a long curved beak. It uses this to dig into the soft earth where it finds earthworms and insects.

e.g. golden plover. The golden plover has a smaller beak. It uses it to snatch for surface insects such as beetles, slugs and fly larvae.

e.g. meadow pipit. The meadow pipit is a common small bird of the moorland ecosystem. It feeds on small insects, especially crane fly.

Primary consumers
e.g. leaf-eating insects

Producers
e.g. lichens and grasses

Decomposers
e.g. earthworms

Soil
Soil moisture
Nutrients

Rock
Nutrients
Groundwater

Key
Living parts of the ecosystem
Non-living parts of the ecosystem

Figure 1 The living and non-living parts (or components) of the treeless tundra ecosystem in Iceland: an example of a biome

How do living things interact with the physical environment?

Ecosystems exist at a variety of scales. The largest, such as tropical rainforests or the treeless tundra of the Arctic region, cover large parts of the Earth. These large ecosystems are known as **biomes**. But ecosystems also exist at much smaller scales, for example salt marshes and sand dunes may cover only a few hectares whilst a garden pond is an ecosystem that is only a few metres across.

In all of these ecosystems complex relationships exist between the living and non-living parts. For example, in a pool such as that at the Wetlands Centre in London, in Figure 2, the water depth varies and this variation provides a variety of habitats. Figure 3 shows that within this ecosystem there is a horizontal structure which is determined by water depth. Variation in water depth (just one non-living part of this ecosystem) provides conditions for different groups of plants. These in turn provide different habitats for various damselflies or dragonflies that are the predators of the insect world in this ecosystem. They in turn may be eaten by birds such as yellow wagtail or hobby (which is a small bird of prey). The dragonfly larvae live underwater and are eaten by fish, frogs, toads or newts. The fish and frogs may be eaten by larger birds such as heron.

Figure 2 A variety of habitats at the London Wetlands Centre is provided by the horizontal structure of the wetland ecosystem

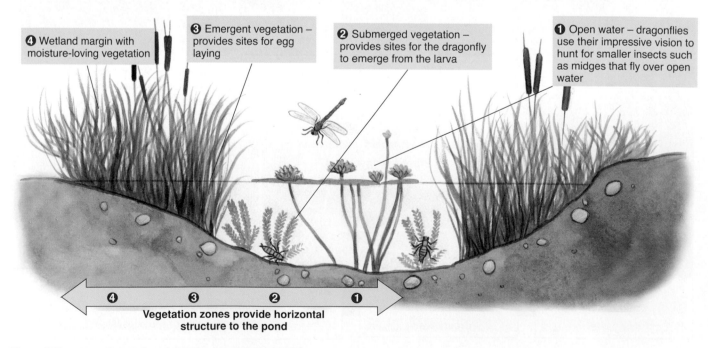

❹ Wetland margin with moisture-loving vegetation

❸ Emergent vegetation – provides sites for egg laying

❷ Submerged vegetation – provides sites for the dragonfly to emerge from the larva

❶ Open water – dragonflies use their impressive vision to hunt for smaller insects such as midges that fly over open water

Vegetation zones provide horizontal structure to the pond

Figure 3 Structure of a pond, and the life cycle of a dragonfly

London — London Wetlands Centre

The London Wetlands Centre in Barnes, south London, has been created on the site of four disused Victorian water storage reservoirs. The reservoirs were designated as a Site of Special Scientific Interest (SSSI) in 1975 because of the large numbers of ducks using the site. The reservoirs were no longer needed, so in 1995 a huge reclamation project began to convert the reservoirs into a 40 hectare wetland ecosystem that would benefit a wide biodiversity. The rectangular reservoirs were originally all the same depth. Engineers partially filled them with earth to create ponds of different sizes, shapes and depths.

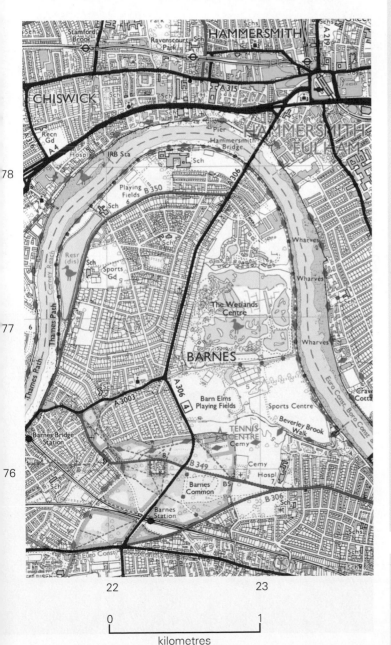

Figure 4 An Ordnance Survey extract featuring the London Wetlands Centre. Scale 1:25,000 Sheet 161

Activity

1. a) Make a sketch of Figure 2.
    b) Pair up the phrases below to make three labels for Figure 2.
        Deeper water with submerged vegetation provides …
        Shallow water with emerging vegetation provides …
        Wetland margin with moisture loving vegetation provides …
        … safe places for wading birds to create their nests.
        … food for diving ducks.
        … sites for dragonflies to lay eggs.
    c) Use Figure 3 to help you decide where each of your three labels should be placed on your sketch.
    d) Explain how the structure of this ecosystem provides a variety of habitats for insects such as dragonflies.

2. Working with a partner, use information from this page to draw a simple food web for a garden pond in the UK.

3. Suggest how each of the following non-living features of a pond might influence a plant, insect or fish living in the pond:
    i) water depth
    ii) water temperature
    iii) amount of light reaching the bottom of the pond
    iv) amount of oxygen dissolved in the water
    v) quantity of fertiliser washed into the pond.

4. Use Figure 4.
    a) Describe the location of the Wetlands Centre.
    b) Give six-figure grid references for:
        i) Hammersmith Bridge   ii) Barnes Station.
    c) Give directions, including distances, for a visitor approaching the Wetlands Visitor Centre (at 226767) on foot from:
        i) Hammersmith Bridge   ii) Barnes Station.
    d) What is the approximate area of the Wetlands Centre?
        i) A little less than 1 km²   ii) A little more than 1 km²   iii) 2 km²

London Wetlands Centre facts and figures

*   The site contains over 30 different wetlands.
*   There are 600 m of boardwalk and 3.4 km of pathway.
*   Over 130 species of wild bird.
*   24 species of butterfly and 260 moths.
*   18 dragonfly and damselfly species.
*   4 species of amphibian.

The global distribution pattern of biomes

Climate is such an important factor in influencing the natural vegetation and wildlife of a region that biomes (the largest-scale ecosystems) broadly match the world's climate zones.

Figure 6 Boreal (or taiga) forest, Finland

Figure 5 Arctic tundra, Iceland

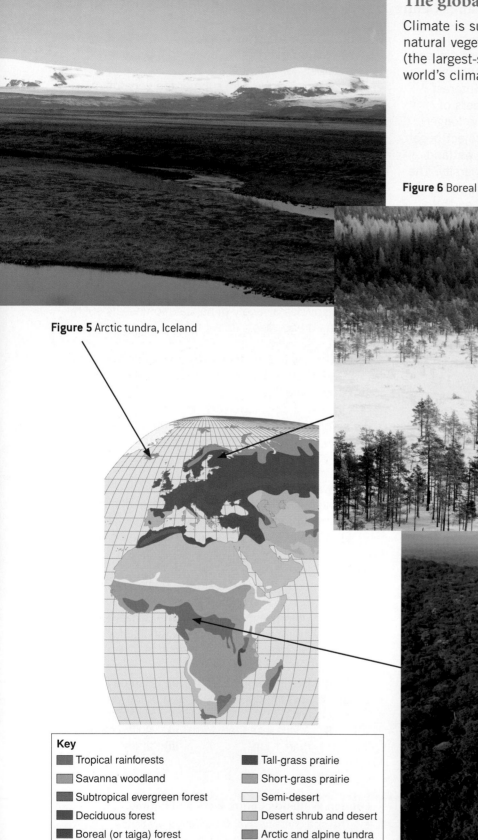

Key

Tropical rainforests	Tall-grass prairie
Savanna woodland	Short-grass prairie
Subtropical evergreen forest	Semi-desert
Deciduous forest	Desert shrub and desert
Boreal (or taiga) forest	Arctic and alpine tundra
Mediterranean forest or scrub	Ice sheet

Figure 7 Biomes of Africa and Europe

Figure 8 Tropical rainforest, Gabon

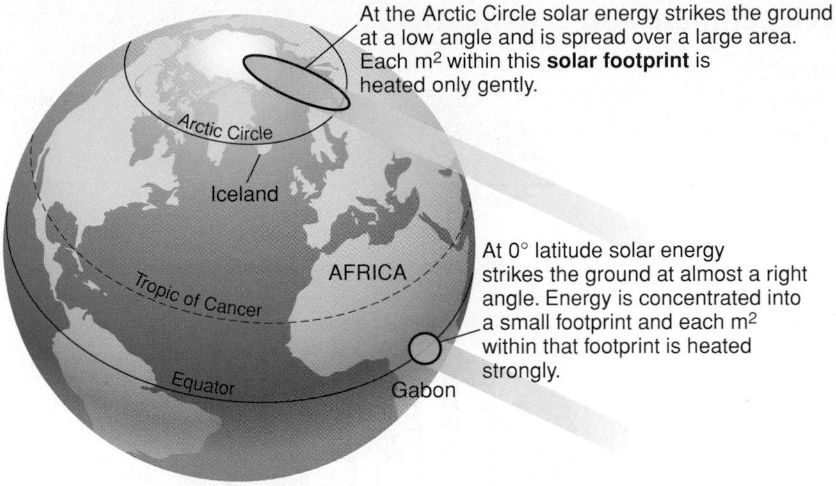
At the Arctic Circle solar energy strikes the ground at a low angle and is spread over a large area. Each m2 within this solar footprint is heated only gently.
Arctic Circle
Iceland
Tropic of Cancer
AFRICA
Equator
Gabon
At 0° latitude solar energy strikes the ground at almost a right angle. Energy is concentrated into a small footprint and each m2 within that footprint is heated strongly.

Figure 9 Solar heating of the Earth varies with latitude

Activity

1 Use Figure 9 to copy and complete the following:
   a) Iceland is just south of ………… whereas Gabon is on the ………… .
   b) The sun strikes the ground in Iceland at ………… whereas in Gabon this angle is much ………… . This means that the sun's energy is more in Gabon.

2 Use Figure 7 to describe the distribution of:
   a) tropical rainforests
   b) boreal forests.

	Tundra moorland 64°N, Iceland		Boreal forest 62°N, Finland		Tropical rainforest 0°N, Gabon	
Month	Temperature (°C)	Precipitation (mm)	Temperature (°C)	Precipitation (mm)	Temperature (°C)	Precipitation (mm)
Jan	–0.5	145	–8.0	38	27.0	249
Feb	0.4	130	–7.5	30	26.5	236
Mar	0.5	115	–4.5	25	27.5	335
Apr	2.9	117	2.5	35	27.5	340
May	6.3	131	8.5	42	26.5	244
Jun	9.0	120	14.0	48	25.0	13
Jul	10.6	158	17.0	76	24.0	3
Aug	10.3	141	15.5	75	25.0	18
Sep	7.4	184	10.5	57	25.5	104
Oct	4.4	184	5.5	57	26.0	345
Nov	1.1	137	0	49	26.0	373
Dec	–0.2	133	–4.0	41	27.5	249

Figure 10 Climate data for three climate stations

Activity

3 Use the climate data in Figure 10 to complete a copy of the following table:

4 Suggest how the differences in climate might affect plant growth in the two forest systems.

	Tropical rainforest	Boreal forest	Tundra moorland
Temperature range			
Months above 10 °C (length of growing season)			
Months below freezing			
Total annual rainfall			
Seasonal variation in rainfall			

Investigating the relationships between climate and ecosystems

Biomes such as the **tropical rainforest** have climatic conditions that promote rapid plant growth. Tropical rainforest trees grow quickly and can reach a height of 40 m or more. Other biomes, like the tundra, have very slow-growing plants that never grow more than a few centimetres high. The differing growth rates of the plants in these biomes can be explained by factors such as the amount of sunlight, length of day, warmth, and amount of water. These factors all depend on either climate or latitude. Read the labels on Figure 11. Notice how the word 'so …' is used to explain how a feature of the climate has influenced plant growth in this ecosystem.

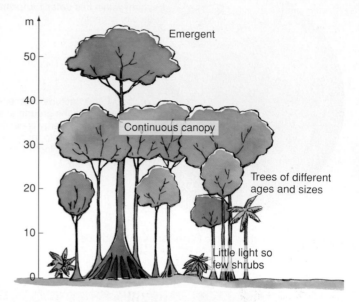

Figure 12 Typical structure of the tropical rainforest

There is plenty of sunlight overhead so plants grow straight and tall

There is plenty of water, sunshine and nutrients so a wide variety of plants are able to grow. This allows a wide diversity of insects, birds and animals

In equatorial regions the temperature is constantly above 25 °C so plants can grow all year and grow quickly.

Figure 11 Tropical rainforest in Reunion, Africa

Figure 13 The treeless arctic tundra in Iceland

Activity

1 Pair up the phrases below to make four sentences that explain the features of the tundra ecosystem in Figure 13.

Temperatures are only above 10 °C (the temperature at which most plants grow) for two or three months so …
Precipitation in the winter months falls as snow, so …
The soils are poor with few nutrients so …
With little shelter the wind can be very strong so …

… plants grow close to the ground where they are less likely to be damaged.
… plants have a long dormant season.
… plants are extremely slow-growing.
… plants have small leaves so they don't lose any moisture.

Nutrient cycles also depend on climate

Plants need minerals containing nitrogen and phosphates. These nutrients exist in rocks, water and the atmosphere. The plants take them from the soil, releasing them back into the soil when the plant dies. This process forms a continuous cycle.

Figure 14 represents nutrient stores and flows in the rainforest ecosystem. The circles represent **nutrient**

stores. The size of each circle is in proportion to the amount of nutrients kept in that part of the ecosystem. The arrows represent **nutrient flows** as minerals move from one store to another. The thickness of each arrow is in proportion to the size of the flow, so large flows of nutrients are shown with thick arrows whilst smaller flows are shown with narrow arrows.

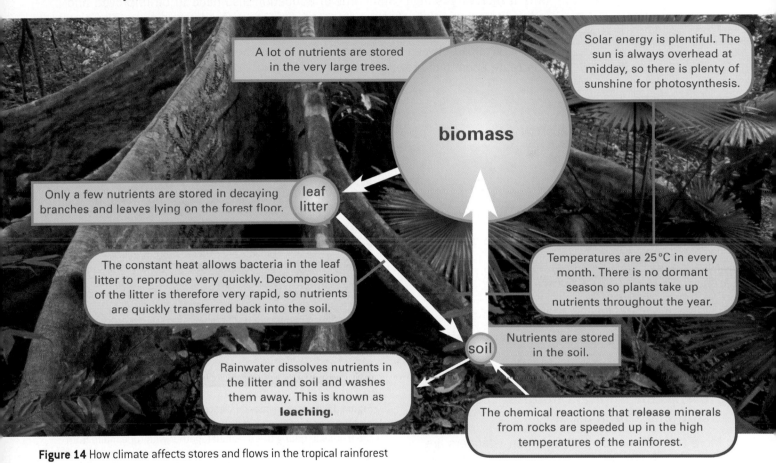

A lot of nutrients are stored in the very large trees.

Solar energy is plentiful. The sun is always overhead at midday, so there is plenty of sunshine for photosynthesis.

biomass

Only a few nutrients are stored in decaying branches and leaves lying on the forest floor.

leaf litter

The constant heat allows bacteria in the leaf litter to reproduce very quickly. Decomposition of the litter is therefore very rapid, so nutrients are quickly transferred back into the soil.

Temperatures are 25°C in every month. There is no dormant season so plants take up nutrients throughout the year.

soil

Nutrients are stored in the soil.

Rainwater dissolves nutrients in the litter and soil and washes them away. This is known as **leaching**.

The chemical reactions that release minerals from rocks are speeded up in the high temperatures of the rainforest.

Figure 14 How climate affects stores and flows in the tropical rainforest

Activity

2 Describe the structure of the tropical rainforest.

3 **a)** Define what is meant by *nutrient stores* and *nutrient flows.*
  b) Describe three places where nutrients are stored in an ecosystem.

4 Study Figure 14.
  a) Describe two ways that nutrients can enter the soil.
  b) Explain why these two nutrient flows are rapid in the rainforest.
  c) Explain why these nutrient flows are likely to be much slower in the boreal forest and tundra.

5 Study Figure 14. Explain why **nutrient cycle** diagrams for the tundra and boreal forest would have:
  a) a larger circle for leaf litter than in the rainforest
  b) a thinner arrow for leaching
  c) a thinner arrow showing nutrient flows into the biomass.

6 Study Figures 11, 12 and 13. Use these, and the information on pages 48–49, to:
  a) describe the main features of each ecosystem
  b) explain the structure of each ecosystem.

How are ecosystems managed?

A case study of logging in the Solomon Islands

The Solomon Islands are a large group of islands in the Pacific Ocean. The natural ecosystem of these mountainous islands is tropical rainforest. The World Bank estimates GNI (per person) to be $730, making this the poorest country in the Pacific region. The country has one of the highest malaria rates in the world and infant mortality is high. Standards of education also need to be improved and adult literacy is relatively low compared with other Pacific countries. The country's economic and social development was crippled by fighting between different ethnic groups between 2000 and 2003. Since then the government has struggled to create economic growth.

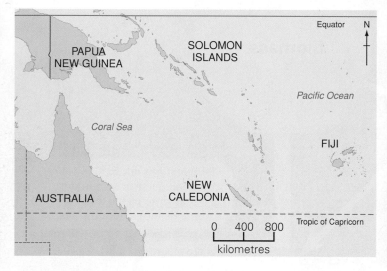

Figure 15 Location of the Solomon Islands

Figure 16 Houses in coastal villages are still built using local materials and traditional methods. Houses are built on stilts using the trunks of young trees lashed together with rope made from vines. They have open windows to take advantage of sea breezes and are thatched using palm leaves from the sago tree

How has the tropical rainforest ecosystem traditionally been used?

More than 80 per cent of Solomon Islanders are subsistence farmers or fishermen. This means they only produce enough food to feed their own families and do not make much profit from their work. The islands are heavily forested and most communities are located around the coastline. The rainforest is still an important resource for villagers. They use it to gather foodstuffs such as fruit, nuts and honey. They also collect leaves, berries and bark to make traditional medicine. For many communities the forest is also an important source of timber not only for building and repairing their homes, but also to build their ocean-going fishing canoes.

Activity

1 Use Figure 15 to copy and complete the following:
**The Solomon Islands are located in the ....
Ocean to the .... of Papua New Guinea.
They are approximately .... km to the
north of New Caledonia. They are between the
Tropic of Capricorn and the ....**

Logging and agri-business

Timber, oil palm and minerals are the main **exports** of the Solomon Islands. Logging is a fast-growing industry. Many **trans-national companies (TNCs)** have recently bought logging rights to fell and export timber from the Solomons.

Most of the timber is exported as unprocessed logs. This means that jobs are not created in the Solomons to process the wood into planks, plywood or furniture – jobs which would help create wealth in this poor country.

China is one of the largest importers of timber from the Solomons. Global Timber, an NGO that monitors the logging trade, estimates that as much as 90 per cent of the tropical hardwood that China **imports** from the Solomon Islands has been felled illegally. Many ecologists are very worried about the damaging impact that this industry is having on the Solomon Islands' fragile environment. They believe that if felling continues at this rate, most of the country's rainforest will have been destroyed by 2020.

Where land has been cleared of forest it has often been converted to oil palm plantations. Huge areas of land that once had a vast diversity of plants and animals now have just oil palms. These plantations are run by internationally owned agricultural businesses (or **agri-business**). These trees produce an oil that can be used in the making of many products, including vegetable oil for cooking, soap, washing powder and bio-fuel (such as bio-diesel for cars).

	Solomon Islands	New Zealand	Fiji
GNI US$	730	28,780	3,800
Under 5 mortality (deaths per 1,000 live births)	73	6	18
Life expectancy	63	80	69
% infants with a low birth weight	13	6	10
% population using improved (safe) drinking water	70	100	47
Maternal mortality: Annual number of women who die from pregnancy-related causes per every 100,000 live births	220	9	210
Adult literacy (% who can read and write)	76	100	96

Figure 17 Development data for selected Pacific region countries. Source: Unicef

Figure 18 Logs felled by a Malaysian TNC are tagged before being exported to Malaysia

Activity

2 **a)** List the ways in which rural communities use the tropical rainforest as a resource.
   b) Explain why this type of use is unlikely to do lasting damage to the ecosystem.

3 **a)** Choose suitable graphical techniques to illustrate the development data in Figure 17. Use your graphs to make comparisons between the Solomon Islands and the other countries.
   b) Explain why the government of the Solomon Islands needs to create jobs and wealth.

4 Explain why converting the rainforest to oil palm plantations concerns many environmentalists.

Is logging sustainable?

The second largest island in the Solomons is Santa Isabel. The communities in North Isabel sold logging rights to a Malaysian TNC. This meant that the land was still owned by the community, but the logging company paid the community for the right to log timber for a fixed period of time. They made various promises to protect the environment during logging. Figures 19 and 20 provide evidence that the TNC operating in Santa Isabel broke these promises. Their poor logging practices have resulted in severe soil erosion, silting-up of rivers, and flooding.

Commercial logging firms such as this TNC make more profit if they work quickly. They use bulldozers to reach the valuable trees. For every tree cut for its timber, it is estimated that 40 or more are destroyed by the heavy machinery. This process destroys trees that have fruit, nuts or medicinal value to the villagers. The villagers have received payments from the TNC, but this amounts to only about 1 per cent of the value of the timber.

Deforestation damages wildlife habitats and often leads to problems of soil erosion. In many cases the logging companies are acting illegally. **Illegal logging** practices include:

- cutting trees without permission
- cutting trees close to rivers where soil erosion can then lead to flooding
- ignoring the rights of local land owners
- paying bribes to local officials
- non-payment of taxes.

Figure 19 A skid-track to remove felled logs has been created on a slope that is far too steep. This has caused soil erosion. The loggers had promised that they would not create this kind of problem

Figure 20 Waste timber from the logging process blocking the Kahigi river. The TNC agreed not to fell trees within 50 m of any major river or 25 m of any minor stream

	Jan	Feb	Mar	Apr	May	Jun	Jul	Aug	Sep	Oct	Nov	Dec
2006	46	51	49	95	61	36	94	53	72	96	50	70
2007	64	111	53	114	115	70	72	83	88	109	58	111
2008	107	36	127	103	107	106	84	135	89	123	82	60
2009	85	111	138	52	109							

Figure 21 Exports of timber (thousand m³) from Solomon Islands to China. Source: www.globaltimber.org.uk/pngsi.htm

Could logging be sustainable?

Logging can provide a better income for local people and not cause long-term damage to the environment. This can be achieved in various ways:

- Only a few trees are felled. If only two trees per hectare are felled every ten years, a rainforest will naturally recover.
- Saplings are planted to replace cut trees.
- Local people fell the tree and process the timber on site using small portable tools.

The Isabel Sustainable Forestry Management Project is one small example. It was funded by aid (450,000 euros) given by the European Union in the mid-1990s. The scheme created skilled labour for local people. Trees are carefully felled to avoid damage to trees of fruit or medicinal value. The timber is then cut into planks in the forest using a portable sawmill. This means that large machines are not needed. It also means that local people add value to the timber, so more profit is retained by the village. This method of processing the timber means that the community keeps about 40 per cent of the finished value of the timber. The project was successful in protecting 17,000 hectares of forest. But the amount of timber produced has been very small.

Figure 22 Members of the Lobi Community in Morovo Lagoon use a portable sawmill to process a freshly felled log into planks. This tree was felled as part of a sustainable eco-forestry programme

Activity

1. **a)** Choose a suitable graph to represent the data in Figure 21.
    b) Describe the trend shown by your graph.

2. Use the text on this page to complete a table like this:

Effects on ...	Unsustainable logging practices	Sustainable logging practices
Soils		
Rivers		
Fruit, nut and medicinal trees		

3. Imagine you could visit the communities affected by commercial logging in Isabel. Discuss what they might tell you about the impact of the TNC on their lives.

4. Explain how the Isabel Sustainable Forestry Management Project is able to:
    a) improve standards of living today
    b) ensure decent standards of living for future generations.

Ecotourism and conservation in Central America

Deforestation creates a major problem for wildlife: the forest becomes fragmented. As clearings get bigger the wildlife is restricted to isolated fragments of forest that are separated by farm land. The animals become trapped in islands of forest surrounded by an ocean of farmland.

The governments of Central America (also known as Mesoamerica) are co-operating with each other in an ambitious conservation project. They want to create a continuous **wildlife corridor** through the length of Central America. The corridors will be created by planting strips of forest to connect the remaining fragments of forest together. The project is called the Mesoamerican Biological Corridor (known by its Spanish initials, CBM) and involves all seven governments of Central America, plus Mexico.

Debt-for-nature swap

Mesoamerica is a **biodiversity hotspot**. It only amounts to 1 per cent of the world's land surface, but it is estimated to contain 7 per cent of the world's terrestrial (land-based) species. Western governments are encouraging conservation in this region by offering **debt-for-nature swaps**. Under these arrangements, the Central American governments agree to spend money conserving ecosystems and wildlife. In return, the Western governments agree to reduce the amount of money that is owed to them. One debt-for-nature swap was made between Costa Rica and the USA. In 2007 Costa Rica agreed to spend $26 million on conservation projects. In exchange, the US government and two non-governmental organisations (NGOs) agreed to buy back a similar amount of Costa Rica's debt.

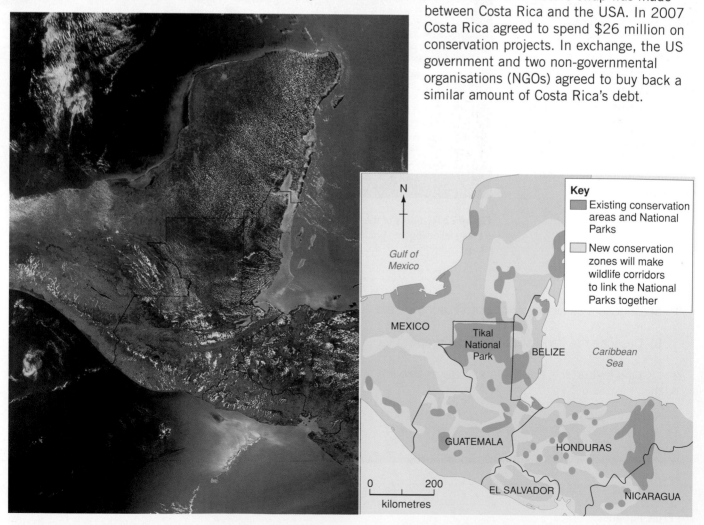

Figure 23 Satellite image of the Mesoamerican Biological Corridor (CBM) project. The red dots show where forest fires are burning

Figure 24 Protected areas (including forest reserves) in Central America and Mexico and the proposed wildlife corridors

Costa Rica

Ecotourism in Costa Rica

The government and businesses in Costa Rica have also encouraged the growth of **ecotourism**. These are small-scale tourist projects that create money for conservation as well as creating local jobs. It is estimated that 70 per cent of Costa Rica's tourists visit the protected environments. In 2000 Costa Rica earned $1.25 billion from ecotourism. One successful example is the creation of a canopy walkway through a small, privately owned part of the Monteverde reserve. Tourists are charged $45 to climb up into the canopy and walk along rope bridges, the longest of which is 300 m long.

Figure 25 The location of Monteverde reserve

Figure 26 The canopy walkway allows visitors to see the birds and other wildlife that live in the canopy of the cloud forest

Country	Protected land as % of total area
Belize	47.5
Costa Rica	23.4
El Salvador	2.0
Guatemala	25.3
Honduras	20.8
Mexico	5.0
Nicaragua	21.3
Panama	19.5

Figure 27 Protected areas (including forest reserves) in Central America and Mexico. Source: Earthlands

Activity

1 Study Figures 23 and 24.
   a) Describe the location of Tikal National Park.
   b) Describe the distribution of forest fires. Do many appear to be burning in conservation areas?

2 Working in pairs, draw a spider diagram to show how fragmentation of the rainforest affects wildlife. Consider the likely impacts of fragmentation on:
   • food chains
   • success of mating
   • predator/prey relationships
   • pollination and seed dispersal.

3 Explain how the new wildlife corridors will help wildlife.

4 Describe the location of the Monteverde reserve.

5 Study Figure 27.
   a) Calculate the average amount of land that is protected in Central America and Mexico.
   b) Present the data in graphical form – include a bar for the average.
   c) How good is Costa Rica's record on conservation compared with that of its neighbours?

6 Suggest how Western governments benefit from debt-for-nature swaps.

Ynyslas, Cerdigion

A case study of management of the sand dunes at Ynyslas, Cerdigion

The Dyfi estuary is a beautiful rural environment that attracts many visitors each year. People visit this part of West Wales for relaxation on the beach or in the dunes or to enjoy a number of leisure activities that include walking, riding, sailing and birdwatching.

The area contains several important and fragile ecosystems which need careful management. One of these is the sand dune system at Ynyslas which is managed by the Countryside Council for Wales.

Figure 28 The changing style of management at Ynyslas

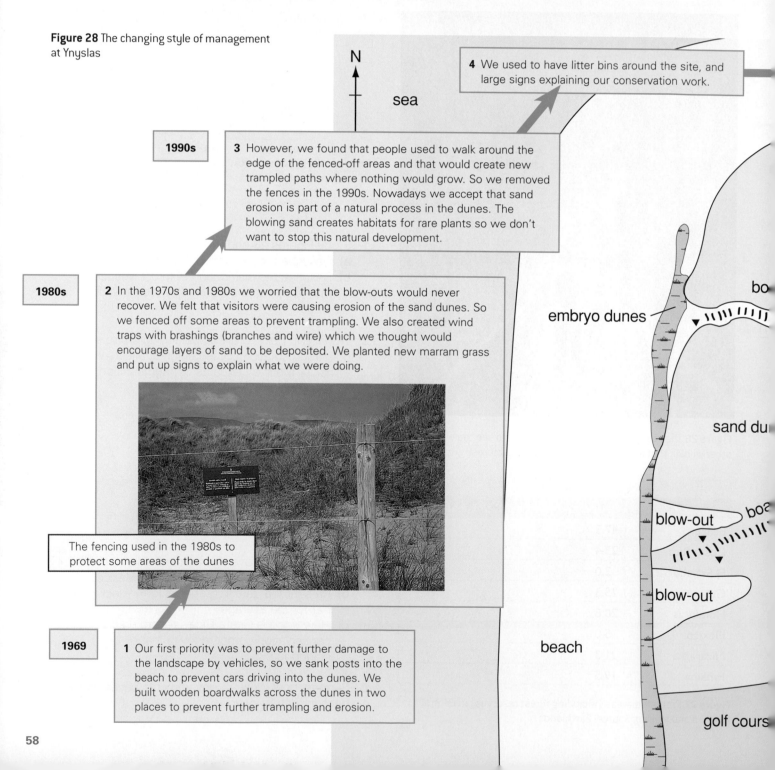

N

sea

4 We used to have litter bins around the site, and large signs explaining our conservation work.

1990s

3 However, we found that people used to walk around the edge of the fenced-off areas and that would create new trampled paths where nothing would grow. So we removed the fences in the 1990s. Nowadays we accept that sand erosion is part of a natural process in the dunes. The blowing sand creates habitats for rare plants so we don't want to stop this natural development.

1980s

2 In the 1970s and 1980s we worried that the blow-outs would never recover. We felt that visitors were causing erosion of the sand dunes. So we fenced off some areas to prevent trampling. We also created wind traps with brashings (branches and wire) which we thought would encourage layers of sand to be deposited. We planted new marram grass and put up signs to explain what we were doing.

The fencing used in the 1980s to protect some areas of the dunes

1969

1 Our first priority was to prevent further damage to the landscape by vehicles, so we sank posts into the beach to prevent cars driving into the dunes. We built wooden boardwalks across the dunes in two places to prevent further trampling and erosion.

embryo dunes

bo

sand du

blow-out

boa

blow-out

beach

golf cours

Activity

1 Study Figure 28. Use it to complete the following table. You should be able to identify at least four issues.

Issue	Management strategy	Evaluation strategy
1		
2		

2 Produce a short report on management at Ynyslas. In it you must identify:
   a) why people visit
   b) the two main aims of the wardens
   c) how and why management strategies have changed
   d) how you think management of the dunes should change in future.

2000s

5 We found that the litter bins used to overflow and rubbish blew about, so we got rid of all the bins.

6 Lots of songbirds live in the dunes including linnet, stonechat, skylark and meadow pipit. We have one area where ringed plovers breed. These small birds nest on the ground and are easily disturbed, so we have fenced off the shingle area where they nest.

7 A lot of rabbits live in the dunes. They keep the grass short and stop it from choking the less competitive flowering plants. The rabbit dung makes the soil much more fertile and as many as 40 different species of flowering plants can grow in just 1 square metre. Also some birds nest in the abandoned rabbit burrows, so we like to have a healthy population of rabbits. However, our neighbour is the golf course. They don't want too many rabbits burrowing into the putting greens and creating damage. So we erected a rabbit-proof fence along our southern boundary. The problem is that this fence now has holes in it and will be costly to maintain.

parking area

posts to prevent cars driving into the dunes

visitor centre

8 In recent years we have enlarged and improved the visitor centre and the boardwalks. Now anyone can easily cross the site to get to the beach. Wheelchair users can access the visitor centre along the boardwalks.

The boardwalk and visitor centre

caravan park

9 One of our biggest management problems today is dog fouling. People are banned from walking their dogs in the summer months on Borth beach to the south. So they come up to Ynyslas to walk their dogs. The problem is that there are very few bacteria in the sandy soil so the dog excrement does not bio-degrade. It lies around for ages and is a nuisance for other visitors.

2009

Pyramidal orchids

What are the likely consequences if ecosystems continue to be damaged?

Are mangrove ecosystems being used unsustainably?

Mangrove forests grow on tropical coastlines. The trees of the mangrove tolerate flooding by both fresh and salt water, so this is both a forest and a wetland, and it supports a very wide range of fish, insects and animals.

Big business regards mangrove forest as useless wasteland. Mangroves are cut down and the swampy land redeveloped. Over 25 million hectares of mangrove forest are estimated to have been destroyed in the last 100 years. The fastest rates of destruction are in Asia. For example, in the Philippines the amount of mangrove declined from 1 million hectares in 1960 to only 100,000 hectares in 1998. Mangrove forests in Central America currently have the second fastest rates of destruction.

Figure 29 Mangroves and cloud forests are two types of tropical forest. Mangroves grow in coastal regions whereas cloud forests grow in mountainous areas

One of the most common reasons for the destruction of mangroves is to convert the land for tourist developments. With their coastal location, mangroves provide a prime location for such things as yachting marinas and hotel complexes. The rapid growth of shrimp (or prawn) farming businesses is another threat to the remaining mangroves. Shrimp farming has grown rapidly over the last 20 years. It is estimated that 1 million hectares of coastal wetlands, including mangroves, has been destroyed in recent years to make the ponds needed by new shrimp farms.

Key
- Cloud forest
- Mangrove forest

N

Mexico

Gulf of Mexico

Cuba

Belize City
Belize
Honduras

Oaxaca
Guatemala City
Guatemala
El Salvador
Nicaragua

Pacific Ocean

Caribbean Sea

Costa Rica
Panama
Colombia
Venezuela

0 — 500 Kilometres

The forest acts as a natural coastal defence. The roots hold the mud together, protecting the land from erosion and reducing the force of large storm waves.

The forest ecosystem supports a range of animals including howler monkeys, deer and armadillo. The canopy provides safe nesting sites for birds.

The wetlands support crocodiles, snakes and crabs. Tropical fish use these sheltered waters as a breeding ground and nursery.

Large prop roots support the tree above high tide. They trap fine sediment carried in the water, causing it to be deposited.

Figure 30 Why mangroves are important to Central American countries

A local fisherman

Local people lose out because they can no longer use the timber or other resources available in the mangrove forest. Local fishermen have noticed a fall in the number of fish they catch. This may be because the mangroves are a nursery ground for young fish. Shrimp farming releases a lot of fertilisers and other chemicals into the environment. Local people sometimes find that their fresh-water wells have become polluted by these chemicals. These are problems that are likely to affect coastal communities for many years after the farms have been abandoned.

Economics expert

Consumer in the UK

The biggest consumers of shrimp (also known as prawns) are the USA, Canada, Japan and Europe. Perhaps consumers will be able to influence what happens to mangroves in Latin America if we demand to know more about how our food is produced. Then we might decide to only buy shrimps or other fish that have been farmed sustainably.

The gains from shrimp farming are often short term. People make quick profits. However, after a few years ponds are abandoned because of disease and pollution. In Asia there are approximately 250,000 hectares of abandoned, polluted ponds where healthy forests once grew. This boom–bust cycle is about to be repeated in Latin America, Africa and the Pacific where shrimp farming is growing in popularity.

Figure 32 Views on whether the use of mangroves for shrimp farming is sustainable

Country	Amount of mangrove forest (hectares)			
	1980	1990	2000	2005
Antigua and Barbuda	1,570	1,200	850	700
Belize	78,500	78,500	76,500	76,000
Costa Rica	63,400	53,400	41,800	41,000
Cuba	537,400	541,400	545,500	547,500
Dominican Republic	34,400	25,800	19,400	16,800
El Salvador	46,700	35,300	28,500	28,000
Guatamala	18,600	17,400	17,500	17,500
Mexico	1,124,000	985,600	885,000	820,000
Nicaragua	103,400	79,300	65,000	65,000
Panama	250,000	190,000	174,400	170,000

Figure 31 Mangrove destruction in selected Central American and Caribbean countries

Activity

1 Describe how mangrove forests provide benefits for wildlife and people.

2 Describe the location of the mangrove forests in Central America.

3 Working in groups, use Figure 31 to investigate the rate of destruction of mangroves in Central America.
   a) Draw a map or series of graphs to represent the data.
   b) Consider each of the following enquiry questions. The data you have may help you to suggest an answer. Discuss what other data you would need to find in order to answer each enquiry fully.
      i) Which countries have the best record for conservation?
      ii) Are countries with larger tourist industries losing mangroves more rapidly than others?
      iii) Are the Caribbean coastlines losing mangroves faster than Pacific coastlines?

4 Study the points of view in Figure 32.
   a) What are the long-term benefits of shrimp farming and who gets these benefits?
   b) What problems does shrimp farming create for people and wildlife?
   c) Do you think shrimp farming is a sustainable use of this ecosystem? Explain your point of view.
   d) Discuss what consumers in the UK can do to help ensure that ecosystems (either mangroves or other ecosystems) are used sustainably.

The Millennium Ecosystem Assessment

The Millennium Ecosystem Assessment (MA) is a scientific report into the state of the environment. Published in 2005, it took five years to write and involved the work of more than 1,360 experts from all parts of the world. The MA concludes that the world's resources have been used to create a better standard of living for billions of people. Ecosystems have been used to supply people with a range of resources including food, clothing, energy and fresh water. However, it also warns that economic activity has done a great deal of damage to the environment.

Millennium Ecosystem Assessment	
1	Modern fishing techniques do not allow fish stocks to recover. The amount of fish in the seas is decreasingly rapidly.
2	The 2 billion people who live in the world's driest areas are increasingly at risk from drought and poverty.
3	We are using up fresh water supplies at a rate that is faster than they can be replaced.
4	Climate change will cause massive problems for many ecosystems.
5	The increasing use of artificial fertilisers and burning of fossil fuels has doubled the amount of nitrogen pollution. This is causing problems in river and marine ecosystems.
6	The destruction of ecosystems (for example, forests, coral reefs and wetlands) is causing the extinction of many species at a scale that is greater than anything seen in the past.

Figure 33 The six main problems identified by the Millennium Ecosystem Assessment

What is the evidence that marine ecosystems are used unsustainably?

One of the key findings of the Millennium Ecosystem Assessment is that the amount of fish in the seas is decreasingly rapidly. If fish are caught faster than the population of fish can reproduce then the fishing industry is unsustainable.

Year	Fish (tonnes)
1986	23
1987	0
1988	0
1989	542
1990	99
1991	158
1992	301
1993	602
1994	656
1995	950
1996	1,004
1997	1,397
1998	1,642
1999	3,163
2000	3,630
2001	4,460
2002	4,400
2003	10,160
2004	11,428
2005	10,858
2006	7,624
2007	7,700

Figure 35 Amount of fish caught (tonnes) in Belize (see Figure 29 for the location of this Central American country)

Activity

1 Study each of the problems listed in Figure 33. Suggest how each of the following economic activities could have contributed to these problems.
   - Agriculture
   - Fishing
   - Mining
   - Timber extraction
   - Manufacturing
   - Tourism

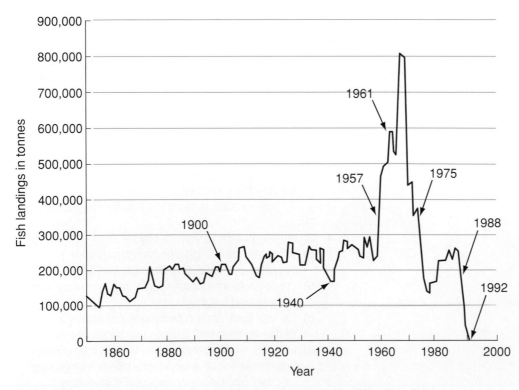

Figure 34 Overfishing caused the collapse of the Atlantic cod stocks off Newfoundland

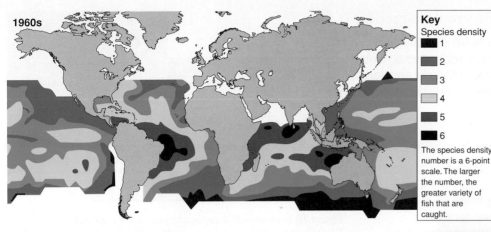

1960s

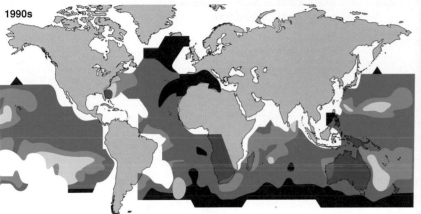

1990s

Key

Species density

1

2

3

4

5

6

The species density number is a 6-point scale. The larger the number, the greater variety of fish that are caught.

Figure 36 Changes in average number of species caught by longline fishing. Longline fishing uses a single line up to 130 km long, which is dragged behind the boat. The line contains thousands of hooks that are baited with scraps of fish such as tuna and swordfish

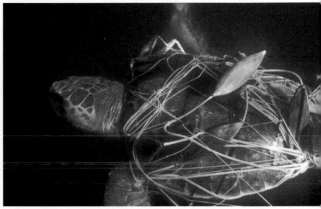

Figure 37 Longline fishing catches and drowns many sea birds and mammals such as turtles. This is known as bycatch

Activity

2 a) Make a sketch of Figure 34.

b) Describe the trend of the cod catch:
  i) up to 1950   **ii)** after 1950.

c) Working in pairs, discuss the labels below. Add these to your copy of the graph in Figure 34 as annotations that explain the trends on the graph.

  A John invests in expensive sonar equipment to find shoals of fish.

  B Tom notices that there are fewer larger (older) fish in the nets.

  C All families use small traditional fishing boats.

  D The Murphy family have to sell their house to repay their debts.

  E The price of locally caught fish rises sharply in the fish market.

  F Some fishing families join up and fight during the Second World War.

  G William finds that his small, traditional boat can no longer compete with the modern trawlers.

d) Suggest how these changes affected people working in the local fishing industry.

3 a) Choose a suitable graphical method to represent Figure 35.

b) What conclusions do you draw from the data in Figures 34 and 35?

c) Is there an alternative explanation for the recent decline in the number of fish caught in Belize?

4 Conservationists are concerned that fish stocks in the North Sea could crash due to overfishing, just like the Atlantic cod crash off Newfoundland. Suggest:

a) two alternative strategies to protect fish stocks in the North Sea from overfishing

b) how fishermen, boat repair yards and fishmongers would be affected by your suggestions.

5 Use Figure 36 and an atlas to describe the changing distribution of fish species caught between the 1960s and 1990s.

Does it matter if ecosystems are damaged?

Sadly logging, oil exploration, intensive farming and over-fishing are all damaging natural ecosystems. But does it really matter if there are fewer forests and less wildlife? After all, farming and fishing provide us with food, jobs and wealth.

Ecosystems provide key services

Scientists argue that ecosystems should be protected and not just for their scientific value. They argue that ecosystems provide people with a number of essential services which they describe as **key services**. Furthermore, they say that these key services have financial value. They include:

- maintaining a steady supply of clean water to rivers
- preventing soil erosion
- reducing the risk of river floods
- providing natural materials such as timber for building, or plants for medicinal use; 75 per cent of the world's population still rely on plant extracts to provide them with medication
- providing foodstuffs such as honey, fruit and nuts.

Conservationists argue that we need to place a greater value on these key services than on the value of the tropical timber alone. The benefit of a clean and regular water supply can be measured in financial terms. Rebuilding homes after a river flood can also be measured financially. The conservationists argue that these key services are more valuable in the long term than the short-term profits gained from logging.

Figure 38 Bees provide a service to humans by pollinating our crops. Beetles also provide a key service. They digest waste materials such as leaf and litter and dung

Figure 39 Key services provided by ecosystems

Provide a safe environment for fish to spawn and juvenile fish to mature, so helping to maintain fish stocks

Tropical rainforests

Provide people with the opportunity to develop recreation or tourism businesses

Coniferous (boreal or taiga) forests

Support thousands of plants and wild animals that contain chemicals that may be useful to agriculture or medicine

Mangrove forests

Inspire a sense of awe and wonder in human beings

Peat bogs/moors

Act as natural coastal defences against storm surges, strong winds and coastal floods

Tropical coral reefs

Soak up rainwater and release it slowly, therefore reducing the risk of flooding downstream

Sand dunes

Act as huge stores of carbon dioxide, so helping to regulate the greenhouse effect

Activity

1 Explain what would happen to our food production without bees and beetles.

2 Using Figure 40:
   a) List the places where water is stored in the rainforest.
   b) Explain how water flows from the atmosphere to the forest and back again.

3 Describe and explain why:
   a) areas of rainforest maintain a steady supply of water for local communities
   b) damaging the structure of the rainforest could affect local people, and people in the wider region.

4 Discuss the six ecosystems in Figure 39. For each ecosystem identify at least one key service (the yellow boxes) that it provides.

5 Write a letter campaigning for the conservation of Central America's cloud forest or mangrove forest. Use information from Figures 39 and 40 to provide evidence of the real value of these key services.

Tropical rainforests regulate water supply

Figure 40 shows how rainforests play an essential role in the regional **water cycle** of tropical areas. The forest acts as a **store** for water in between rainfall events. After a rainstorm it is thought that about 80 per cent of the rainfall is transferred back to the atmosphere by evaporation and transpiration. This moisture condenses forming rain clouds for the next rainstorm. So rainforests are a source of moisture for future rainfall events.

At least 200 million people live in the world's tropical rainforests. This includes the tribal groups, or **indigenous peoples**, of the rainforest. Many more people live downstream of the rivers that leave these forests. The forest maintains a constant and even supply of water to these rivers. If the rainforest water cycle were to be broken then the water supply of many millions of people could be put at risk. The total amount of water flowing in the rivers would be reduced and the supply would become more uneven with periods of low water supply punctuated by sudden flooding.

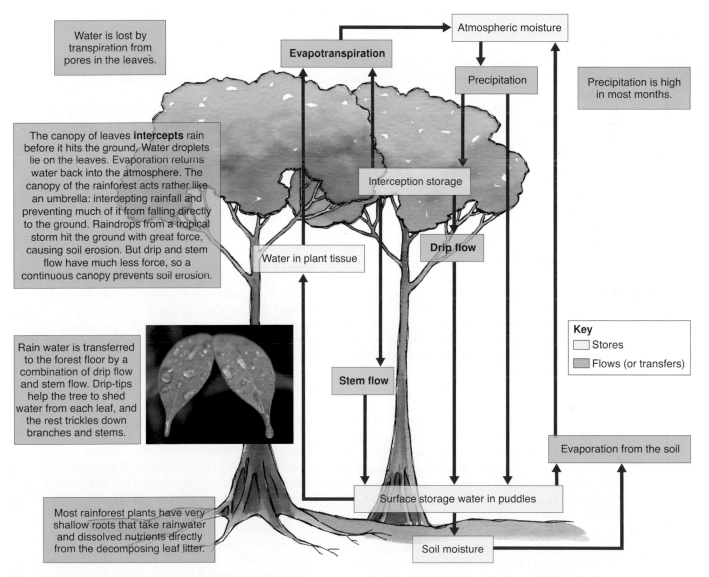

Figure 40 The water cycle in a tropical rainforest

Understanding marking schemes

When you read a question it is important that you think about what you are being asked to do. If a question is worth 6 or 8 marks it is important for you to think about the structure of your answer and plan an answer that will address all parts of the question. These questions will be marked using a levels marking scheme. You will achieve an A* if you include detail, use correct geographical terminology and include case studies.

Generally, questions worth fewer than 6 marks will be marked using a point marking scheme. You will score 1 mark for every relevant point that is made. In the shorter questions always look to develop points to score 2 marks for each point made. To develop points made remember the three Es:

• Give examples
• Expand points made
• Explain the point.

Mark Scheme

Level One (1–3 marks) Limited knowledge of named ecosystem. Little understanding of the concept of sustainability. Candidate outlines a small range of measures adopted to promote sustainable use of the ecosystem.

Level Two (4–6 marks) Clear knowledge of named ecosystem. Clear understanding of the concept of sustainability. Candidate describes a range of measures adopted to promote sustainable use of the ecosystem.

Level Three (7–8 marks) Clear and detailed knowledge of named ecosystem. Clear understanding of the concept of sustainability. Candidate describes a wide range of measures adopted to promote sustainability and gives named examples to support the answer given.

Sample questions

Study Figures 6–9 on pages 48 and 49.
a) Use the resources to outline the nature of the tropical rainforest ecosystem.   [4]
b) Describe how an ecosystem that you have studied can be managed in a sustainable way?   [8]

Student answer

(a) The vegetation of the rainforest is very lush. ✓ You are not able to see the ground in the photograph because of the canopy ✓ of trees. There is no free space for other vegetation than trees in the rainforest. The rainforest is found in Africa near the equator ✓ in countries such as Gabon. ✓

(b) The ecosystem that I have studied is the tropical rainforest. This is found around the world with places which have an equatorial climate. The rainforest provides the most luxuriant vegetation found on Earth. The Amazonian rainforest is the largest rainforest in the world. However due to demands for timber from logging companies and land for cattle ranches the forest is disappearing at an alarming rate. Trees such as mahogany take hundreds of years to regrow and once chopped down may be lost forever. One way to stop the rainforest disappearing is to use selective logging where trees are measured and felled only when they reach a certain height. The Forest Stewardship Council only allows timber sold to come from sustainable logging. Today as people look for more exciting holidays are going to the rainforest for their holiday, this is known as 'ecotourism'.

What the examiner has to say!

Answers are marked using a points marking scheme. The candidate correctly describes the vegetation as lush and expands on this with evidence from the photograph. The location of the ecosystem near the equator in Africa is given a mark and an example of Gabon develops this point. The answer scores the maximum 4 marks.

What the examiner has to say!

This question requires an extended answer and is marked using a levels mark scheme (see above). This answer has a good structure and evidence of planning. The tropical rainforest is identified and relevant background material included. However the candidate spends too long on this background information. The overall answer demonstrates understanding of the concept of sustainability and gives two examples of measures that could be adopted to manage the forest. The answer lacks detail and case study knowledge, with the exception of noting the role of the Forest Stewardship Council, needed for level 3. This answer is worth 6 marks, at the top of level 2.

Why does the nature of tourism differ between one place and another?

What factors affect the nature of tourism?

What do you want from a holiday? Some people want to relax on a beach, while others are looking for excitement and adventure. Some people want to visit museums and historical sites whilst others might want to see wildlife or go bird watching. Each holiday destination has its own distinctive climate, landscape, culture and heritage, so these become the factors that affect the nature of tourism in that place.

| Mexico | Cancun is the largest tourist resort in the Yucatan peninsula of Mexico. It is a classic example of **mass tourism**. In other words, a huge number of jobs have been created by the massive numbers of tourists arriving on relatively cheap package holidays. Around 3 million tourists visit the resort each year, which includes just over 2 million foreign tourists. |

Figure 1 A street vendor selling fruit, Cancun – one example of how tourism can boost employment indirectly

Figure 2 The beach at Cancun

Activity

1 Working with a partner:
   a) Suggest what factors make Cancun such a popular resort.
   b) Make a list of the kinds of jobs that are created by tourism:
      i) directly (people employed to provide a service to the tourists)
      ii) indirectly (an existing job which benefits because of the arrival of tourists).

What factors affect the nature of tourism in the Yucatan?

The Yucatan is a large peninsula of land that juts out of Central America into the Caribbean Sea. It is mostly occupied by the Mexican state of Quintana Roo with the small tropical country of Belize in the south-eastern part of the region. The Yucatan has a lot more to offer than just the traditional attractions of sun, sea and sand. The eastern coastline has the second longest **barrier reef** in the world, providing excellent opportunities for diving and other water sports. Wildlife enthusiasts can explore rainforests, watch turtles and go bird-watching. The Yucatan is also famous for the archaeological remains of the Mayan civilisation which collapsed mysteriously in 1441, leaving behind stunning temples and pyramids in the Yucatan's rainforest.

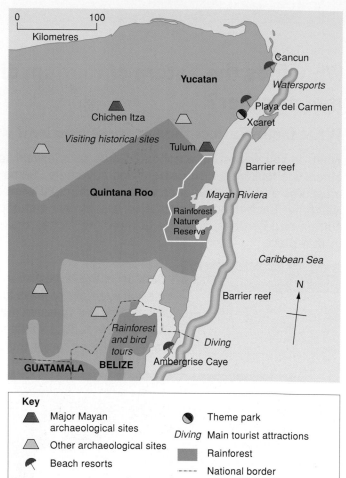

Figure 4 Tourist attractions of the Yucatan

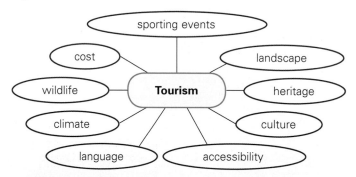

Figure 3 The factors that affect the nature of tourism

Figure 5 Remains of the Mayan civilisation are scattered throughout the Yucatan

Figure 6 Tourists swimming with dolphins at Xcaret

The resort of Cancun was the brainchild of FUNATOR, the Mexican National Tourism Development Agency, which believed that a new mass tourist resort would create massive **positive multiplier effects** in the regional and national economies. The agency examined both the Pacific and Caribbean coastlines carefully before choosing this site as the best place to build the brand new resort. It chose a long **spit** of sand in the Yucatan. There was nothing but a tiny fishing village here until the 1970s. The first hotel opened in 1974, and the resort has grown rapidly ever since.

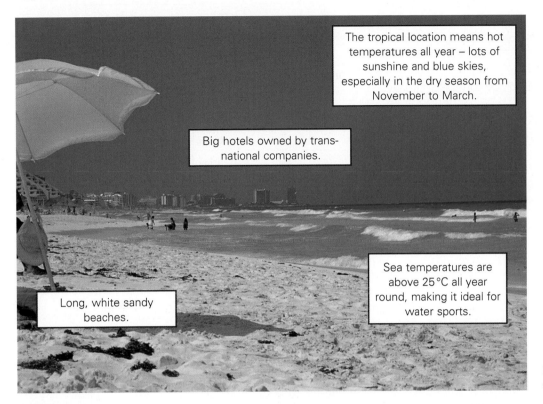

The tropical location means hot temperatures all year – lots of sunshine and blue skies, especially in the dry season from November to March.

Big hotels owned by trans-national companies.

Sea temperatures are above 25 °C all year round, making it ideal for water sports.

Long, white sandy beaches.

Figure 7 Factors influencing visitor numbers to Cancun

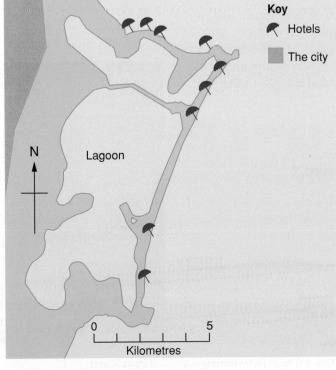

Key

☂ Hotels

▩ The city

Lagoon

N

0   5
Kilometres

Figure 8 Map of Cancun

Activity

1 Use Figure 4 to describe the location of Cancun.

2 a) Explain why FUNATOR wanted to develop Cancun.
   b) Make a copy of Figure 3. Add labels explaining why FUNATOR chose Cancun as the site for its new resort.

3 A student has annotated Figure 7. Two of these labels explain the factors that affect the nature of tourism better than the other two.
   a) Identify which are the better annotations and explain your choice.
   b) Suggest how the other two labels could be improved.

4 Study Figures 1 to 8. Create a piece of promotional material (a poster, podcast or leaflet) advertising holidays in the Yucatan to a specific group of people (e.g. young families or backpackers).

How does security change people's attitudes to travel?

Tourists need to feel safe and secure. A health scare, such as the swine flu pandemic of 2009, or violence and unrest, can seriously damage a country's tourist industry.

Activity

1 a) Choose a suitable technique to represent the data in Figure 9.
   b) Describe the trend of your graph.
   c) The hurricane season is an annual event that reduces tourist arrivals. Swine flu was a one-off event. Do some research and add annotations to your graph that fully explain the two troughs in the trend of this graph.

2008	May	183,377
	June	200,400
	July	206,242
	August	174,701
	September	106,713
	October	121,341
	November	151,356
	December	192,500
2009	January	212,323
	February	216,449
	March	223,945
	April	184,331
	May	63,606
	June	134,501

Figure 9 Tourist arrivals to Cancun in Mexico, 2008–9. Source: Caribbean Tourism Organisation

Lebanon   Case study of Lebanon

Lebanon is a small, mountainous country at the eastern end of the Mediterranean Sea. It has a Mediterranean climate with hot, dry summers and mild winters. The sandy beaches are a natural attraction for visitors in the summer. In the winter visitors are attracted to the mountains where there is plenty of powder snow for downhill skiing, snowboarding and cross-country skiing. All year round visitors can enjoy the many historical and cultural sites such as the ancient cities of Jbail (Byblos), Saida (Sidon) and Sour (Tyre).

During the 1960s Lebanon was a popular tourist destination. It was known as 'The Switzerland of the Middle East'. But violence and conflict during the 1970s and 80s made Lebanon much too dangerous for tourism (see Figure 11). Tourism has grown steadily as foreign visitors recognise that the country is now stable and safe to visit. Arrivals in Lebanon grew from 740,000 in 2000 to 1,400,000 in 2008.

Lebanon has a complex recent history of violence:

- During the 1948 Arab–Israeli war, Palestinians fled to Lebanon. They were unable to return. There are an estimated 40,000 Palestinians living in refugee camps in the Lebanon.
- Between 1975 and 1990 a civil war was fought in Lebanon during which 150,000 people were killed and another 200,000 wounded.
- In 2000, Israeli soldiers who had occupied southern Lebanon since 1982 were withdrawn. At this point Lebanon began to be seen as a safer, more stable country.
- In 2005 the former prime minister was assassinated by a car bomb. The incident led to massive demonstrations in which ordinary people demanded that 15,000 Syrian troops (who occupied part of the country) must withdraw.
- In 2006 Palestinian fighters launched rockets from southern Lebanon into Israel.
- In 2007 there was fighting between Lebanese soldiers and Palestinians in a refugee camp in northern Lebanon. 40,000 people fled the fighting.

Figure 11 Fact file: Conflict in the Lebanon

Figure 10 Greco-Roman ruins in Tyre

- Travel to some areas of Lebanon requires caution. We advise against all travel to Palestinian refugee camps and against all but essential travel to south of the Litani.
- Although the situation overall in Lebanon is calm, it is fragile. On several occasions in recent years, the security situation has deteriorated quickly. Anyone travelling to Lebanon should keep themselves well informed and closely monitor political and security developments.
- There is a high threat from terrorism in Lebanon. Attacks could be indiscriminate, including in places frequented by expatriates and foreign travellers such as hotels and restaurants.

Source: www.fco.gov.uk/en/travelling-and-living-overseas/travel-advice-by-country/middle-east-north-africa/lebanon

Figure 12 Travel advice in 2009 from the Foreign and Commonwealth Office

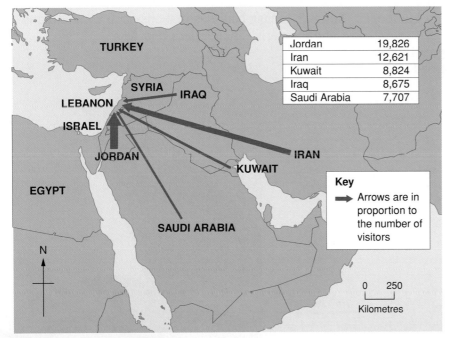

Jordan	19,826
Iran	12,621
Kuwait	8,824
Iraq	8,675
Saudi Arabia	7,707

Figure 13 Visitors to the Lebanon from neighbouring countries, June 2009

Country	Number of visitors
France	10,107
Germany	8,836
Sweden	7,040
Denmark	4,605
UK	3,714
USA	21,126
Canada	16,735
Brazil	2,656

Figure 14 Origin of visitors to Lebanon, June 2009. Source: Lebanese Tourist Board

2007	41,2041
2008	47,3574
2009	76,1415

Figure 15 Number of visitors to Lebanon (six-month totals from January to June). Source: Lebanese Tourist Board

Activity

2 Describe three factors that determine the nature of tourism in Lebanon.

3 a) Using Lebanon as an example, explain why jobs in the tourist industry depend on good security.
  b) Suggest two different strategies that the Lebanese government could use to increase the number of tourist visitors.

4 Use Figures 13, 14 and 15:
  a) Use suitable techniques to represent the data in Figures 14 and 15.
  b) Describe and explain the patterns shown in this data.

How and why is tourism changing?

Patterns of tourism are changing rapidly. The way we travel, the distance we travel and the frequency of our holidays are all changing. These changes are largely to do with changing technologies. In particular, there has been a huge growth in air travel as aeroplanes have become faster and larger. At the same time air travel has become much cheaper, so more people can afford to fly more often. The cost of flying fell particularly steeply during the 1990s when there was a massive rise in the number of airline companies offering cheap flights. These are known as **budget airlines**. UK budget airlines typically offer frequent, cheap flights to other airports in the UK (internal flights) or to other **short-haul** destinations in Europe. The low cost of these flights has encouraged customers to take several short breaks a year rather than just one annual two-week holiday abroad.

Another trend that has had an impact on tourism has been the rapid growth of communication technologies. It is now much easier for people to discover what tourist attractions are available in distant places than ever before. People now have access to a wealth of information on the internet which was not available before the 1990s. Changes in the media have also made it easier to find out about holidays in distant places. Up until the early 1990s everyone in the UK only had four TV channels. Now travel programmes are accessible on multiple channels on their TVs due to online, cable and satellite broadcasting. This has made it much easier for people to research and book holidays to **long-haul** destinations such as South and Central America, Australasia and Asia.

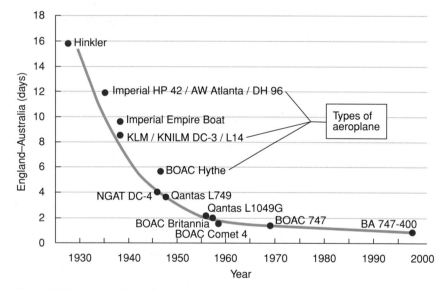

Figure 16 Changes in flight time between London and Australia

Figure 18 Aeroplanes such as a Boeing 777 allow relatively quick travel to long-haul destinations

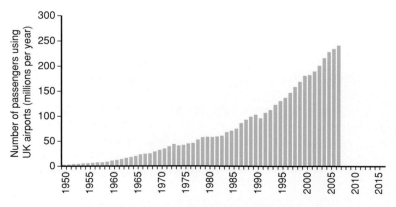

Figure 17 The number of passengers (millions) travelling through UK airports, 1950–2007

Activity

1   Use Figure 16 to describe and explain how the time it takes to get to Australia has changed.
   Study Figure 17.
   a) Describe how the number of people using UK airports changed:
      i)   between 1950 and 1983
      ii) between 1983 and 2007.
   b) Use evidence from the graph to predict how many passengers could be using UK airports by 2015.

GIS Activity: Eurostat and Defra

http://epp.eurostat.ec.europa.eu

Eurostat is the official website for statistics that cover the members of the EU. Use this weblink to go to the home page. Then, on the right of the screen, follow the link to Country Profiles (which has a thumbnail map of the EU) to get to the GIS. Figure 19 is an example of the kind of map you can produce.

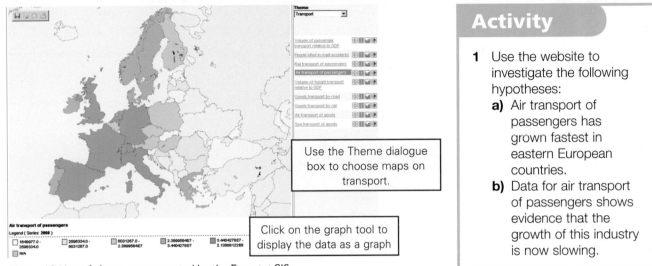

Use the Theme dialogue box to choose maps on transport.

Click on the graph tool to display the data as a graph

Figure 19 Map of air transport created by the Eurostat GIS

Activity

1   Use the website to investigate the following hypotheses:
    a) Air transport of passengers has grown fastest in eastern European countries.
    b) Data for air transport of passengers shows evidence that the growth of this industry is now slowing.

GIS Activity: Defra Noise Mapping England website

http://services.defra.gov.uk/wps/portal/noise

Researching noise nuisance

Noise is a nuisance to people living under flight paths close to airports. The government believes that noise levels will stay similar to those of today, even as the number of planes increases, because newer planes are quieter. Defra, which is a government department, has mapped noise levels around the airports of England. Figure 20 shows the area immediately to the east of Heathrow.

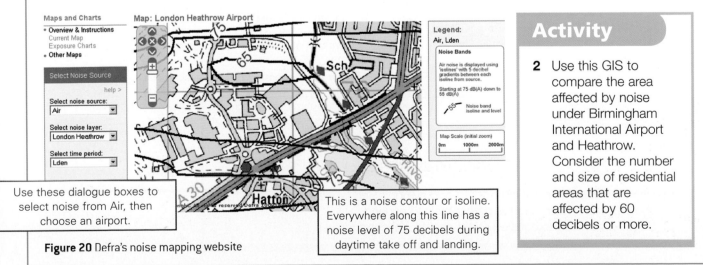

Use these dialogue boxes to select noise from Air, then choose an airport.

This is a noise contour or isoline. Everywhere along this line has a noise level of 75 decibels during daytime take off and landing.

Figure 20 Defra's noise mapping website

Activity

2   Use this GIS to compare the area affected by noise under Birmingham International Airport and Heathrow. Consider the number and size of residential areas that are affected by 60 decibels or more.

Geography Futures

The future of air travel

The growth of air travel, for business and tourism, has economic and environmental impacts. Environmental campaigners are concerned about the emission of carbon dioxide from air travel which adds to the **greenhouse effect**. They also oppose the expansion of airports. Those who work in the aviation industry point out that the growth in the number of flights is good for the UK economy as more foreign tourists visit the UK. They say we need new runways so that more planes can use UK airports.

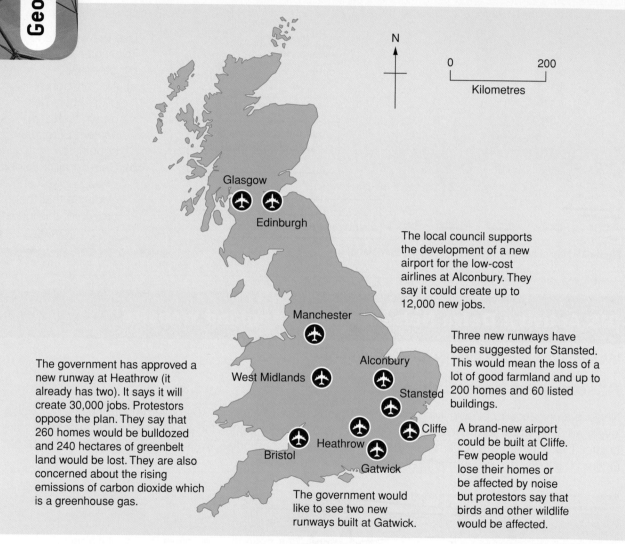

The local council supports the development of a new airport for the low-cost airlines at Alconbury. They say it could create up to 12,000 new jobs.

Three new runways have been suggested for Stansted. This would mean the loss of a lot of good farmland and up to 200 homes and 60 listed buildings.

The government has approved a new runway at Heathrow (it already has two). It says it will create 30,000 jobs. Protestors oppose the plan. They say that 260 homes would be bulldozed and 240 hectares of greenbelt land would be lost. They are also concerned about the rising emissions of carbon dioxide which is a greenhouse gas.

A brand-new airport could be built at Cliffe. Few people would lose their homes or be affected by noise but protestors say that birds and other wildlife would be affected.

The government would like to see two new runways built at Gatwick.

Figure 21 UK airports where expansion is being considered

Activity

1 Study Figures 21 and 23.
   a) Draw a sketch map of south-east England and show the location of the airports.
   b) Use the information in Figure 23 to add symbols and labels to your map to show by how much each airport is likely to expand.
   c) Suggest how this expansion might affect local communities.

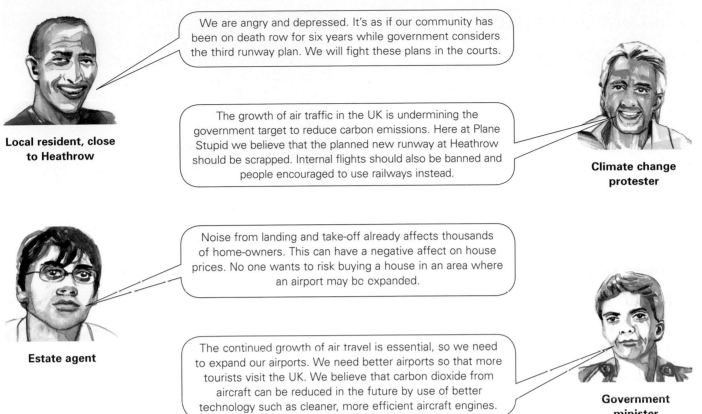

Local resident, close to Heathrow

We are angry and depressed. It's as if our community has been on death row for six years while government considers the third runway plan. We will fight these plans in the courts.

Climate change protester

The growth of air traffic in the UK is undermining the government target to reduce carbon emissions. Here at Plane Stupid we believe that the planned new runway at Heathrow should be scrapped. Internal flights should also be banned and people encouraged to use railways instead.

Estate agent

Noise from landing and take-off already affects thousands of home-owners. This can have a negative affect on house prices. No one wants to risk buying a house in an area where an airport may be expanded.

Government minister

The continued growth of air travel is essential, so we need to expand our airports. We need better airports so that more tourists visit the UK. We believe that carbon dioxide from aircraft can be reduced in the future by use of better technology such as cleaner, more efficient aircraft engines.

Figure 22 Opposing views on the growth of air travel and the expansion of UK airports

Airport	2005	2015	2030
Heathrow	65	80	135
Gatwick	35	35	40
Stanstead	20	35	55
Luton	10	15	15
London City	2	4	5
Total for all London airports	**132**	**169**	**250**
Other UK airports	93	139	203
Total for all UK airports	**225**	**308**	**453**

Figure 23 Predicted growth in the number of passengers using UK airports (millions of people per year).
Source: www.dft.gov.uk/pgr/aviation/atf/co2forecasts09/co2forecasts09.pdf

Activity

2 Study Figures 21 and 22.
   a) Outline the arguments for and against expanding existing airports.
   b) Sort your arguments under these headings:
   environmental   economic   social

3 Would it be better to expand Heathrow or build a new airport to the east of London? Use the resources here, and the internet, to research these options. Create a poster that persuades people to support whichever you think is the better idea.

What are the impacts of tourism?

Iceland

Is tourism good or bad for Iceland?

The waterfall at Gullfoss (which means 'Golden Falls') is one of Iceland's main tourist attractions. It has more than 300,000 visitors a year. Gullfoss and nearby Geyser are a little over one hour from Reykjavik by road. Many people come by coach as part of a tour of the 'Golden Circle' region. There is no fee to visit the waterfall itself, but visitors contribute in many ways to the local economy by:

- spending money in the large café and gift shop
- paying for a coach trip from Reykjavik (about £45 in 2009)
- hiring a car to visit the area
- staying overnight in one of the many local hotels and guesthouses
- eating in a local restaurant
- paying for a flight over the falls in a light aircraft
- paying for a local leisure activity such as whitewater rafting or horse riding.

Figure 25 Tourists at Gulfoss waterfall

All of this creates a lot of employment and business opportunities for local people. For example, many local farmers have converted their buildings to large guesthouses or have opened riding stables. The money earned by local people is then spent in local shops and businesses. This is an example of the **positive multiplier effect**.

Not all of the impacts of tourism are good for Iceland and its people. The peak of the tourist season to Iceland's rural areas is from June to August. Fewer people visit in the winter when it is only light for a few short hours. Employment in the hotels is seasonal and most people need a second job when there are fewer tourists.

The Golden Circle, which is the closest rural region to Reykjavik, has become popular with tourists from Reykjavik as well as with foreign tourists. Many are buying second homes here. There is a danger that local people could feel swamped by newcomers. In just one housing development at Grimsnes, close to Gullfoss, there are over 1,500 new holiday homes in a rural community that has only 356 permanent residents.

The sheer number of visitors can also cause problems such as footpath erosion at **honeypot sites** such as Gullfoss. Steps and paths have to be managed carefully if they are to be safe and not look an eyesore. Off-road driving in the rural regions of Iceland is popular, but the tyre tracks and deep ruts are scarring the landscape. The Environment and Food Agency of Iceland is so concerned about this damage that most off-road driving has been banned since 1999.

Figure 24 A light aircraft takes tourists for a sightseeing flight over Gullfoss waterfall

Iceland is just south of the Arctic Circle so the growing season is short. Plants damaged by off-road vehicles grow back very slowly.

Undamaged landscapes have a **wilderness** quality because they are unspoiled by human activity.

Soils are volcanic and very loose. Tyres easily dig deep ruts.

Where plants have been damaged the soils are easily eroded by wind and rain.

Tyre tracks are an unnatural feature in Iceland's landscape.

Figure 26 Illegal off-road driving in Skaftafell National Park has left these tyre tracks

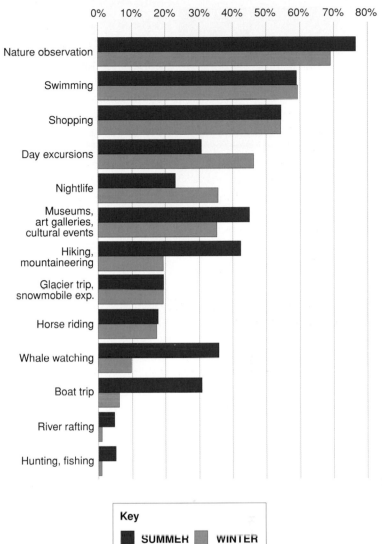

Figure 28 Main leisure activities of tourists to Iceland

Key
■ SUMMER   ■ WINTER

(Bar chart activities, top to bottom: Nature observation, Swimming, Shopping, Day excursions, Nightlife, Museums, art galleries, cultural events, Hiking, mountaineering, Glacier trip, snowmobile exp., Horse riding, Whale watching, Boat trip, River rafting, Hunting, fishing)

Figure 27 Footpath erosion at Seljalandsfoss, another tourist attraction in the Golden Circle

Activity

1 Use Figures 24 and 25. Work in pairs to make a list of ten words that describe how people might be affected by experiencing this landscape.

2 Use Figure 28.
   a) Suggest why nightlife and day excursions (coach trips to places like Gullfoss) are more popular in winter.
   b) Suggest why whale watching and boat trips are more popular in summer.
   c) List the leisure activities that are linked to landscape.

3 Explain why it is important for Iceland's government to protect the country's dramatic landscape.

Mexico

The social costs of tourism in Cancun

Tourism certainly has created many jobs in the Yucatan, but what are its wider effects for local people? In Cancun the hotel zone is separate from the local community: a design known as a **tourist enclave**. Whilst the tourists stay in air-conditioned comfort in their hotels, the workers travel home to **shanty housing** in Puerto Juarez which is one hour away by bus. Local people aren't even allowed on the beaches. The beaches are owned by the state, but controlled by the hotels. They keep local people away to prevent tourists from being hassled by vendors who try to sell food, drinks or their services as guides.

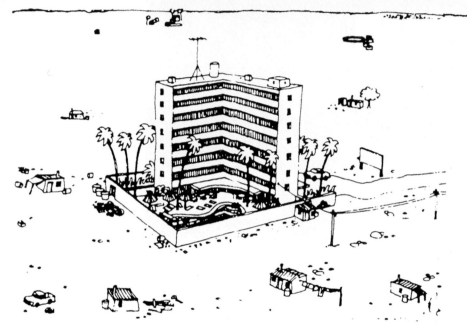

"Dear George, here we are in the middle of things having a great time. We feel we're really getting to know this exotic country..."

Figure 29 Tourist enclaves

The buses have been imported. They take tourists to foreign-owned hotels which serve a lot of imported food and drink.

Most airlines that carry the tourists are owned by foreign trans-national companies (TNCs).

Figure 30 Where does the money go?

A report by Tourism Concern concludes that working conditions for workers in the tourism industry in Cancun are poor. Many earn only US$5 for working a 12- to 14-hour day. Many workers in the large hotels are only offered short, temporary contracts. This means that workers can be laid off at the end of a one- or three-month contract if the seasonal pattern of visitors means there is insufficient work.

The contrast in wealth between tourists and the local community can create conflict and frustration. Local teenagers grow up expecting to enjoy similar consumer goods to those they see being enjoyed by the tourists, but they can't always afford them. Shops sell imported foods, soft drinks and clothing but these are often more expensive than local products and are too expensive for local people to buy.

Figure 31 Views on the development of tourism in Cancun

> I can't afford a decent home. I live in a rented shack. It costs $80 a month. I share the outside toilet with neighbours and the tin roof leaks when it rains heavily. The tourists have everything they need, but we have no space or leisure facilities. We're not even allowed on the beach!

Hotel worker

> In resorts like Cancun and the Maya Riviera, the cost of living is very high and is not matched by wages. Average salaries are rarely above $4 a day, while a flat of one or two rooms in Playa can cost $150 a month.

Campaign worker for Tourism Concern
(who campaign on tourism and human rights issues)

> We use security guards to keep locals off the beach. The problem is that some 'beach boys' hassle the tourists. They try to sell fast food or souvenirs. Sometimes there have been problems with drug dealers and even muggings.

Hotel manager

Figure 32 In a shanty town close to Cancun, the bar advertises a TNC soft drink

> Many people who work in the hotels of Cancun are migrants from other parts of Mexico. They suffer because they are separated from their families and original communities. Most of them are badly paid and rely on tips to make up their wages. Many work long hours and have stressful working conditions. Some suffer from alcohol or drug abuse.

Social worker

Activity

1 Discuss:
   a) what you consider to be the advantages and disadvantages of mass tourism for the local people and economy of Yucatan
   b) the reasons for the governor of Quintana Roo trying to change the image of the resort of Cancun
   c) the advantages and disadvantages of allowing part of the Yucatan barrier reef to become a 'sacrificial reef'.

2 Study Figure 29.
   a) Suggest a suitable caption for this cartoon.
   b) Justify the view that enclaves are bad for both tourists and local people.
   c) Suggest why Cancun was developed as an enclave.

3 Discuss the points of view in Figure 31.
   a) Sort the issues raised (for example, one heading you could use would be *Income*).
   b) What are the main causes of these issues?
   c) Suggest possible solutions to one of these issues.

How can tourism be developed in a sustainable fashion?

Ideally, tourism should be sustainable, meaning that it should have long lasting benefits. However, for tourism to be developed in a sustainable fashion it needs to satisfy several conflicting needs. These are summarised in Figure 33.

Figure 33 The conflicting demands of sustainable tourism

Local people need to benefit. This may take the form of new jobs and better pay. Where poverty is widespread it should also provide better basic services such as clean water, sewage treatment systems and schools for local people.

The environment (including wildlife/ecosystems) should not be damaged so much by the growth of tourism that it cannot recover.

The growth of tourism should not create problems for future generations of local people. For example, if the development of tourism uses more clean water than can be replaced by natural processes then tourism is unsustainable.

The growth of tourism should not create so many problems that tourists soon stop coming (because the environment has been spoilt).

Activity

1 Use Figure 33 to outline at least two different ways in which tourism in Cancun has failed to be sustainable.

2 Suggest how the Governor of Quintana Roo should plan tourist developments in the Yucatan over the next ten to twenty years. Give reasons for your choices.

Learning lessons from the Yucatan

There is evidence that the development of mass tourism in Cancun during the 1970s and 80s caused problems for local people and the environment. During the building of the resort, thousands of **mangrove** trees were cleared from the lagoon to make room for yacht marinas and water sports. By the late 1990s it was obvious that the lagoon was badly polluted by sewage and with oil spilled from the boats. The barrier reef along the coastline was also getting damaged. Coral reefs are very fragile and slow-growing. They are vulnerable to diseases caused by sewage in the sea. They are also easily broken when divers stand on the reef, or when the anchors of dive boats are dragged across the corals.

Fearful that tourists would stop coming if the environment was spoilt, the governor of Quintana Roo has insisted that more effort must be made to protect the environment. New hotels have to meet higher standards of energy and water conservation. The most popular snorkelling and diving area off Cancun was designated as a National Marine Park. Despite this there are still so many divers that damage to the reef's **ecosystem** is inevitable. Biologists now refer to this area as a 'sacrificial reef'. They think it's better to concentrate the divers here rather than let them spread out onto other sections of the reef which are currently visited less and are in better condition.

Figure 34 Very strict laws prevent tourists from taking coral souvenirs out of Mexico. This street vendor is selling coral and sharks' teeth to visitors to Cancun

Keeping tourists in their zone: a strategy in Tyre, Lebanon

The Tyre coast in southern Lebanon is Lebanon's largest and best preserved sandy beach. The Lebanese government would like to encourage tourism, but recognises that mass tourism would conflict with the needs of local people and would damage a fragile environment. One potential conflict here is over water. It is estimated that tourists to the Mediterranean use between 300 and 850 litres of water per person per day: tourist uses of water include cleaning processes such as laundry in hotels, and washing-up in restaurants. By contrast, water use in Lebanon is estimated to be 200 litres of water per person per day. The Tyre region relies on natural supplies of groundwater. This supply is **recharged** from water that seeps slowly down into the rocks from melting snow in the mountains (see Figure 36). There is very little recharge from rainfall in the long dry summers when demand from both tourism and local farmers is high.

The Tyre coast also includes a number of fragile ecosystems that would be easily damaged by the development of tourism. These include beaches that are nesting sites for endangered loggerhead and green sea turtles. The sand dunes and wetlands behind the beach are also home to frogs, insects, several rare plants and animals such as the Arabian spiny mouse. The area has been protected since 1998 when a Nature Reserve covering 380 hectares was created. Tyre Coast Reserve is cut into two segments by the Rashidieh refugee camp. The reserve itself has been zoned into different land uses with the highest levels of protection being placed on the conservation zone.

Activity

3 Explain why water resources need to be considered when deciding whether a planned tourist development is likely to be sustainable.

4 Use Figure 35.
   a) Describe the location of the tourist zone.
   b) Explain why this zone has been separated from each of the other zones.

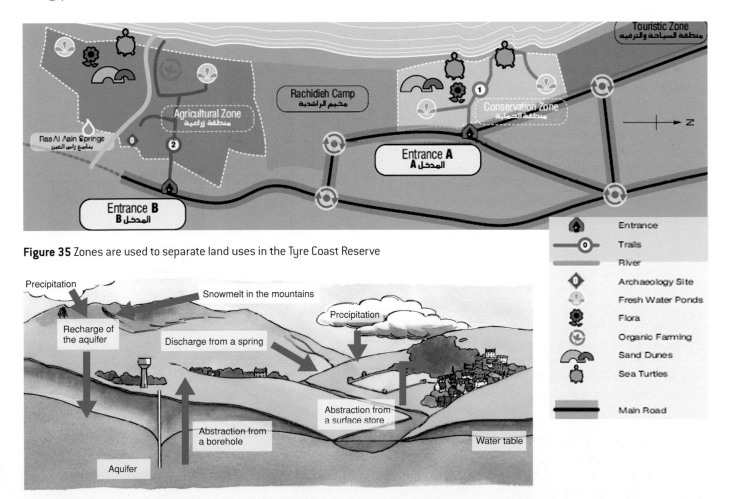

Figure 35 Zones are used to separate land uses in the Tyre Coast Reserve

Figure 36 What will happen to the level of the water table if groundwater is abstracted faster than it is recharged?

South Africa   Is sport tourism the solution?

Events such as the Olympic Games and Football World Cup cost millions to stage. So why are countries so keen to hold these events? The answer is to do with the huge benefits that can be created by a new trend in tourism: the growth of sport tourism. For example, the Sydney Olympics in 2000 cost £2,252 million to stage but earned £5,558 million. Of this total, £2,443 million came from tourism. New jobs will be created directly in the tourist industry, for example employment in hotels, restaurants and bars. In addition, new jobs will be created indirectly in occupations that support the tourists, such as taxi driving. Staging a major sporting event has other benefits too. By staging the Olympics in London in 2012 the government hopes to regenerate a run-down inner urban area of the city. Massive investments in new infrastructure such as roads and sports facilities have transformed the area.

It is hoped that staging the World Cup in South Africa in 2010 will help regenerate ten urban areas. The benefits for South African cities will be:

- New sports facilities: While cricket and rugby are mainly played by white South Africans, football is the favourite sport of black South Africans. The new sports facilities will provide a **legacy**: improved sporting facilities that can be used by South Africans for many years after the 2010 World Cup.
- New image: South Africa is hoping to create a positive image amongst visiting fans and in the media. The 2002 World Cup was shown on TV in over 200 countries. A total of 1.1 billion people watched the final. If people think that South African cities are attractive, exciting places, then they may return here on holiday or even invest money in local businesses.
- New jobs: In the short term the regeneration project will create thousands of jobs for local people in construction. This should have a positive multiplier effect. The extra jobs mean extra income, which means extra spending in local shops and services. In the longer term, more visitors to South Africa will create more jobs in tourism.

	South Africans	Foreign tourists	FIFA officials and sponsors
Average spend per day (£)	62	115	144
Average length of stay (days)	2	16	8

Figure 37 Predicted amount of money spent by visitors to South Africa's World Cup.

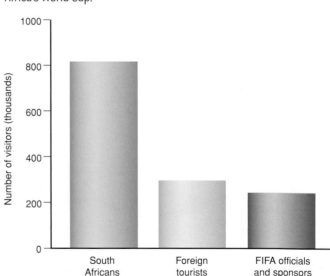

Figure 38 Predicted number of visitors to South Africa's World Cup

Activity

1 a) Choose a suitable graphical technique to represent the data in Figure 37.
   b) Calculate the average amount of money spent by each type of visitor over the whole length of their stay.
   c) Use the data in Figure 38 to predict the total amount of money spent by each of the three types of visitor.

2 Outline the advantages of staging the Football World Cup for South Africa. Sort the advantages:
   a) before the games
   b) during the games
   c) after the games.

3 Use Figure 39 to create a programme for a football fan visiting South Africa in 2010. The fan wants to see matches at three different grounds and visit a National Park. Give directions for the fan, making sure you clearly describe the location of each place that is visited.

Examiner's Tips

Describing locations

To describe a location means to be able to pinpoint somewhere on a map. Describing a location on an Ordnance Survey map can be done easily by giving a grid reference. But describing a location on a map that has no grid lines requires a different technique. To describe the location of places on Figure 39, which has no grid lines, you will have to use other significant places on the map, places that really stand out such as Pretoria, Lesotho or Kruger National Park, as landmarks to guide the viewer to the place you are describing.

First, you need to give a broad indication of place by describing in which part of the map the viewer should be looking. Always use points of the compass, such as 'in northern South Africa' rather than 'at the top of the map'. Second, you should use a combination of two facts to pinpoint a specific location:

- Distance from a landmark using km.
- Direction from a landmark using points of the compass.

Describing distributions

To describe a distribution is to describe how similar things are spread across a map. Geographers are interested in the distribution of natural features such as forests, volcanoes or habitats, as well as human features such as settlements, hospitals or sporting facilities.

Describing a distribution requires you to do two things. First, you need to describe where on the map the features are located. Second, you need to describe any pattern the features might make: regular, random or clustered.

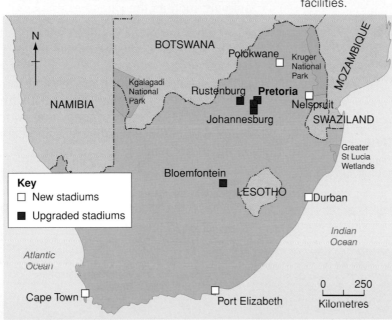

Key
☐ New stadiums
■ Upgraded stadiums

Figure 39 The location of the 2010 World Cup football grounds

Activity

4 Describe the location of:
   a) Cape Town
   b) Pretoria.

5 Describe the distribution of National Parks in South Africa.

a) Describe the location of Polokwane.   [3]
b) Describe the distribution of World Cup cities in South Africa.   [4]

Student answer

a) Polokwane is in northern South Africa.✓ It is approximately 250 km✓ north-east of Pretoria✓ and 200 km✓ west of Kruger National Park.✓

Student answer

(b) Six of the ten cities that are going to host the world Cup are in northern South Africa✓, with two in central and eastern regions✓ and two in the south.✓ The cities are scattered fairly randomly✓ across South Africa, although there is a cluster of World Cup cities around the capital Pretoria.✓

What the examiner has to say!

This is an excellent answer! The candidate makes five clear points about the location of Polokwane and scores a maximum 3 marks.

What the examiner has to say!

This is another very good answer! The candidate makes five clear points and scores a maximum 4 marks. I am impressed with the use of the terms 'random' and 'clustered'.

Could hunting save Africa's wildlife?

Limpopo is the most rural of South Africa's nine provinces. Most people have farm occupations and most farm workers are poorly paid; many earn less than a US$1 a day. The average household income is below 1,000 Rand (US$140) and 60 per cent of families live below the poverty line.

Wild animals such as giraffe, zebra, wildebeest and impala are common in many parts of Limpopo. Tourists visit the region to go on safari and see this spectacular wildlife. Some of these animals are so common that they are **culled** so that they don't compete with cattle for grazing. Scientists monitor wildlife populations and decide each year how many wild animals should be shot to keep the population stable.

Activity

1 Describe the distribution of conservation areas in Limpopo.

2 Explain why it is important to diversify the economy in districts like Waterberg.

3 Explain how an ecotourism project in Limpopo:
   a) improves standards of living
   b) conserves wildlife.

The Waterberg Biosphere Reserve was created in 1999. The Reserve contains 75 mammal species (including elephant, rhinoceros and giraffe) and 300 species of bird, while 77,000 people live in the reserve. The dry climate makes farming difficult and incomes are low. Some farmers in this area are diversifying their income by switching to ecotourism. This means that tourists pay to stay with local families or in lodges on larger farms. Local people are employed to act as guides and wardens. Some of the money that is earned from ecotourism is paid directly into conservation projects. These include breeding programmes for endangered animals, habitat conservation and anti-poaching patrols to protect animals such as the rhino.

As in other parts of Limpopo, scientists believe that a cull of some wild animals is needed so that land is not over-grazed, so a limited amount of hunting is allowed. Tourists pay a daily fee and then a 'trophy fee' for each wild animal they shoot with a rifle or cross-bow. Much of this money is paid to the land owner who can use it to protect and care for wildlife on his or her land.

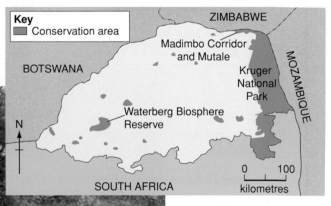

Figure 40 Conservation areas in Limpopo

Figure 41 This tourist will have paid about £165 for a day's hunting (2009 prices). On top of that he has had to pay a 'trophy fee' for each animal he kills. This kudo has a trophy fee of £1,060

Hunting is good for conservation. I used to have cattle on my farm but my land was getting over-grazed. I have switched to ecotourism and trophy hunting. I take tourists for walking safaris. I also allow some hunting. My business is more profitable now. I love wildlife! I look after my wildlife because it is my main source of income.

White South African landowner

There are over 900 hunting farms in Limpopo. They bring in over R500 million (£42 million) a year in trophy fees. Tourism and hunting are creating jobs and wealth for a poor region of South Africa.

Government minister

We support 'trophy hunting' as a means of managing wildlife as long as it is scientifically monitored. We recognise that it can be used to help create sustainable development of some rural communities.

WWF spokesperson

Figure 42 Views on trophy hunting

Activity

4 Discuss the views on trophy hunting in Figure 42.
   a) List the main arguments for and against trophy hunting.
   b) As a group, prepare a presentation or poster to persuade people that trophy hunting is either a good or a bad development for Limpopo.

Trophy hunting is a sport for rich men. The hunters are not conservationists. They just like killing animals. In some cases even endangered animals like leopards are killed as long as the fee is high enough.

Anti-hunt protestor

I know some people who are employed as trackers and guides. However, most ordinary South Africans do not benefit from 'trophy hunting'. It is the wealthy land owners who keep most of the profit.

Black South African farmer

GIS Activity: Planning a holiday using the South African Tourist Board website

www.southafrica.net/sat/content/en/za/home

Activity

1 If you have access to ICT use this website to plan a three-centre holiday for a tourist who:
   a) wants to see wildlife
   b) is interested in adventure and sport.
2 Use ICT to prepare a short presentation about the holiday that you have planned.

Figure 43 Screenshot from the South African Tourist Board

Iceland

Activity

1 Study Figure 45.
   a) Describe the distribution of regions that have lost most people.
   b) Describe which parts of Iceland are gaining population.
   c) Explain the pattern you have identified in answers a) and b).

Can sustainable futures be created from tourism in rural Iceland?

The West Fjords is the most remote part of Iceland from Reykjavik. Most tourists to Iceland visit Reykjavik, where nightclubs are an attraction, or the South West where the main attraction is the Blue Lagoon spa. Many tourists also visit the rural area known as the 'Golden Circle' in the south region (see page 76). Far fewer tourists visit the more remote parts of Iceland.

The traditional rural economy of the West Fjords is in decline. Fishing has always been the biggest employer, but the government has cut the number of fish that can be caught in order to conserve fish stocks in the sea. Sheep farming is the second biggest employer, but it is unprofitable and unpopular among the young.

Each year the rural regions of Iceland receive some migrants and lose others. In some regions more people leave the region than move in, a situation known as **net out-migration**. The loss of people by migration, combined with low birth rates, is causing **rural depopulation.** Depopulation of the West Fjords is causing serious concern. If rural populations become too small then essential services such as schools and doctors' clinics become increasingly inefficient and expensive to sustain. If a doctor's surgery closes, local people find that they are further and further away from health care. Rural communities could become **unsustainable** and have no future.

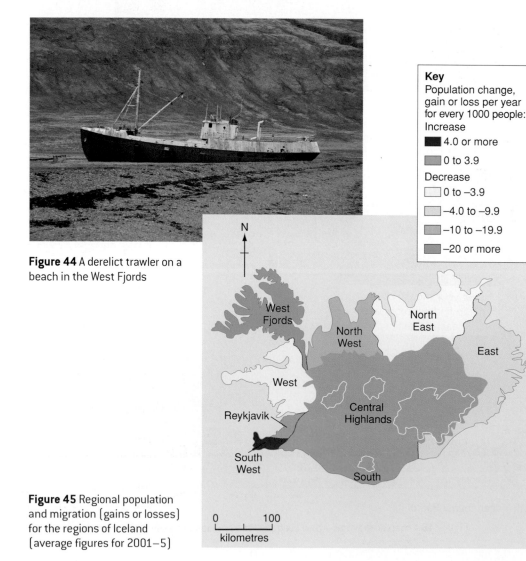

Figure 44 A derelict trawler on a beach in the West Fjords

Key
Population change, gain or loss per year for every 1000 people:
Increase
■ 4.0 or more
▨ 0 to 3.9
Decrease
☐ 0 to −3.9
▨ −4.0 to −9.9
▨ −10 to −19.9
▨ −20 or more

Figure 45 Regional population and migration (gains or losses) for the regions of Iceland (average figures for 2001–5)

0   100
kilometres

1986	14.1
1987	17.8
1988	31.1
1989	27.7
1990	18.4
1991	23.4
1992	9.8
1993	16.0
1994	28.6
1995	47.9
1996	40.7
1997	44.6
1998	39.4
1999	43.5
2000	29.1
2001	21.2
2002	23.0
2003	16.7
2004	27.6
2005	39.2
2006	33.4

Figure 46 Net out-migration from West Fjords, 1986–2006 (figures per 1,000 population)

Whale watching creates jobs and can continue without damaging the environment, so it is an example of a sustainable development for rural communities in Iceland. Iceland has a long tradition of whale hunting but many people support an end to whaling if jobs are created in nature-based tourism instead. Apart from whale watching, the West Fjords has much to offer tourists interested in the natural environment:

• sea or river fishing
• bird watching
• kayaking, horse riding and hiking in the summer and skiing in winter.

Iceland's government believes that new industries such as tourism must be encouraged in order to **diversify** the rural economy. The West Fjords Development Agency (Atvest) is attempting to diversify the rural economy by promoting tourism to the region as well as trying to attract high-tech industries such as data processing, specialised food processing and fishing-related industries. The Northern Periphery Programme gives European Union money to projects in the remote regions of Arctic countries. One of its projects is called Saga Lands. This project is being used in the West Fjords to develop facilities for tourists who are interested in the Viking heritage and culture of the region.

Figure 47 Whale watching helps to sustain rural communities in Iceland

Activity

2 Explain how depopulation can affect rural services such as clinics, schools and post offices.

3 **a)** Choose a suitable technique to graphically represent the data in Figure 46.
   b) Is the depopulation issue getting worse? Use evidence from your graph.

4 Use Figure 48 and an atlas.
   a) Name four countries.
   b) Describe the distribution of these countries.

5 Explain how projects such as Saga Lands (Viking culture) or whale watching create jobs both directly and indirectly in the rural community.

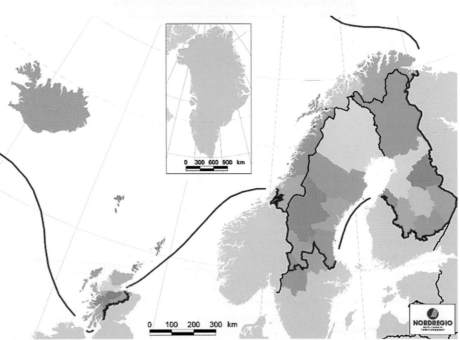

Figure 48 A map of the region that qualifies for development assistance from the Northern Periphery Programme

Geography Futures

Creating sustainable rural communities

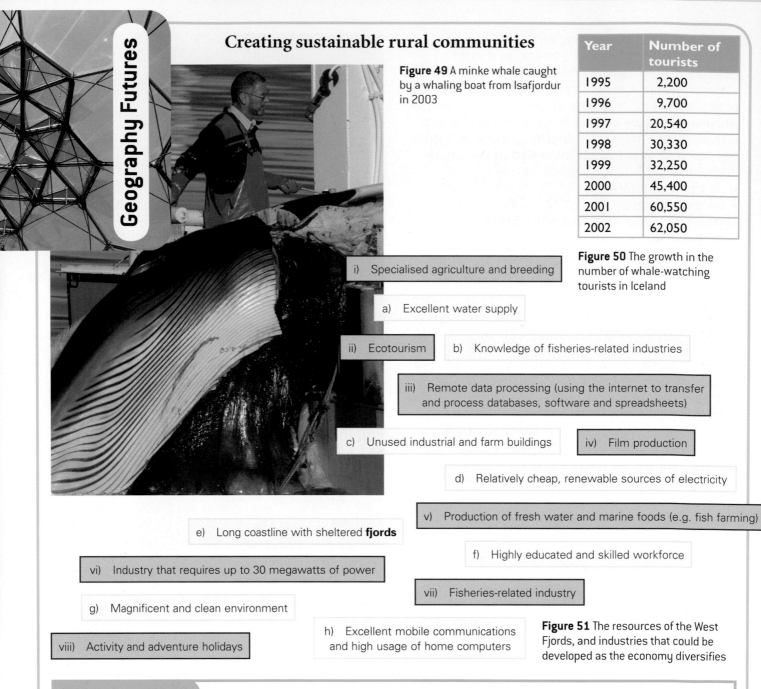

Figure 49 A minke whale caught by a whaling boat from Isafjordur in 2003

Year	Number of tourists
1995	2,200
1996	9,700
1997	20,540
1998	30,330
1999	32,250
2000	45,400
2001	60,550
2002	62,050

Figure 50 The growth in the number of whale-watching tourists in Iceland

i) Specialised agriculture and breeding

a) Excellent water supply

ii) Ecotourism

b) Knowledge of fisheries-related industries

iii) Remote data processing (using the internet to transfer and process databases, software and spreadsheets)

c) Unused industrial and farm buildings

iv) Film production

d) Relatively cheap, renewable sources of electricity

v) Production of fresh water and marine foods (e.g. fish farming)

e) Long coastline with sheltered **fjords**

f) Highly educated and skilled workforce

vi) Industry that requires up to 30 megawatts of power

vii) Fisheries-related industry

g) Magnificent and clean environment

viii) Activity and adventure holidays

h) Excellent mobile communications and high usage of home computers

Figure 51 The resources of the West Fjords, and industries that could be developed as the economy diversifies

Activity

1 a) Choose an appropriate graphical technique to represent the data in Figure 50.
   b) Describe the trend of your graph.

2 Suggest the point of view of each of the following to both whale hunting and whale watching:
   a) A member of Greenpeace in the UK.
   b) The owner of a whaling boat in Isafjordur, which is the largest settlement in the West Fjords.
   c) The owner of a hotel in Isafjordur.

3 Explain why it is important for the rural economy of Iceland to diversify.

4 Study Figure 51.
   a) Match the West Fjords' resources a)–h) to potential industries that could be attracted to the region i)–viii).
   b) Use your list to describe how you think the West Fjords should diversify its economy. Suggest the possible advantages of your scheme compared with alternative types of diversification.

In what different ways are European city centres being renewed?

Figure 1 The new St David's Shopping Centre, opened in Cardiff in 2009

Towns and cities are dynamic – they are changing rapidly. Planners and architects are planning for today and tomorrow, with a view to improving our lives through renewal and development. We see it happening all around us, like the changes taking shape in Cardiff city centre (see Figure 1). Some of the changes are at the early stage of planning as designers play with ambitious plans to create sustainable and green cities for the future.

Figure 2 shows four cities where major projects are underway.

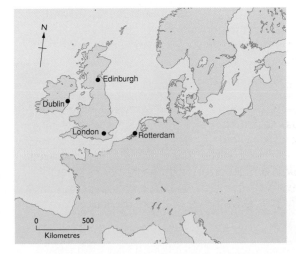

City	Project	Website and search words
Dublin (Ireland)	A town centre regeneration project	www.springcross.ie or search using 'Ballymun Town Centre regeneration'
London (UK)	Regeneration of the city through sport	www.legacy-now.co.uk or search using 'The legacy of the London Olympics'
Edinburgh (UK)	Improving transport, improving city life	www.edinburghtrams.com or search using 'Edinburgh Trams back on track'
Rotterdam (Holland)	A city for tomorrow – residential and commercial regeneration	Search using 'Kop van Zuid project'

Figure 2 Selected cities across Europe with major development projects

Is my city like your city?

I'm proud of my city. It's a great place to live. In recent years the city has changed dramatically. In my travels across the country I see similar changes occurring in other cities like Cardiff and Manchester, and even on the continent in cities like Lille (France) and Bielefeld (Germany). The map in Figure 3 shows just a few of the changes made in my city in recent years.

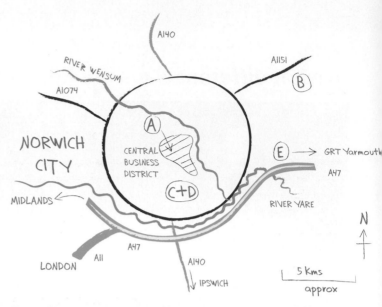

Figure 3 Urban change in Norwich

Activity

1 Ask your friends and relatives about the changes that have taken place in a city near you. Were all the changes for the better?

Recent renewal projects in Norwich

A Norwich is in the top ten for shopping facilities in the UK. Two huge shopping centres have been designed to complement the medieval heart of the city. Find out more at:
www.visitnorwich.co.uk/norwich-shopping-centres.aspx

Activity

2 Figure 3 is an ideal sketch map. It has an indication of scale and compass direction; it is clear and concise; it shows a clear distribution. Draw a sketch map to show urban change in a city or town near you.

B The government has announced the development of 4 eco-communities to lead the way in sustainable development. One will be situated north-east of Norwich. Find out more at:
www.rackheatheco-community.com

D Norwich is now a vibrant centre for nightlife. The Riverside Centre is at the heart of a growing leisure and entertainment district. Find out more at:
www.riversidecentrenorwich.co.uk

C Norwich is making the most of reclaiming former industrial sites. The Riverside Housing development has been constructed on decontaminated land close to the city centre. Find out more at:
www.norwich.gov.uk/webapps/atoz/service_page. asp?id=1268

E With its medieval core, Norwich, like many European cities, faces acute traffic problems. The introduction of an extensive Park and Ride scheme is one way to tackle the problem. Find out more at:
www.norwich.gov.uk/webapps/atoz/service_page. asp?id=1481

Who would be a planner?

Planners make bold statements about the future. In England and Wales they work with elected councillors to produce a Local Development Framework (LDF). They offer solutions to solve existing problems and develop ideas for a better future. The statements below are typical of what appears in many LDFs.

> Our vision is to improve the quality of life for all who live in, work in, learn in and visit the city, by supporting growth and making sure that development happens in a sustainable way so that the facilities enjoyed by local people are not harmed and the town is improved.
> By 2025 we will live in a more vibrant, active and attractive modern city which successfully combines modern development with historic character. It will be a place where people want to live, work, learn, visit and invest – and it will have a reduced carbon footprint.

Figure 4 A planner introducing the LDF

Activity

3 What would you say to your local planners to make sure that the views of teenagers are represented in the LDF? As a starting point, use the ideas put forward by teenagers in a Newport school (Figure 6) when planners visited their geography class.

The spider diagram (Figure 5) shows just a small number of the factors that planners need to consider when shaping the LDF. An important part of the process is to consult with local people about their feelings.

Public open space · Landscape and wildlife issues · Work and employment issues · Housing needs · Cultural provision · Transport issues · **What do planners need to consider when shaping their LDF?** · Waste disposal · Crime/Policing issues · Shopping services · Education opportunities · National and regional government plans · Leisure facilities

Figure 5 What do planners need to consider when shaping their LDF?

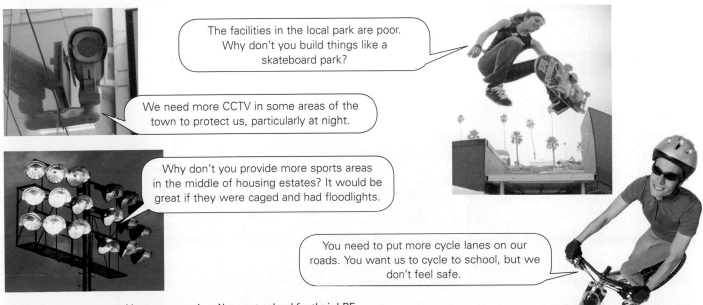

The facilities in the local park are poor. Why don't you build things like a skateboard park?

We need more CCTV in some areas of the town to protect us, particularly at night.

Why don't you provide more sports areas in the middle of housing estates? It would be great if they were caged and had floodlights.

You need to put more cycle lanes on our roads. You want us to cycle to school, but we don't feel safe.

Figure 6 Ideas suggested by teenagers in a Newport school for their LDF

Ipswich

Urban change – too good to be true?

Ipswich is one of the fastest-growing towns in the UK. Figure 7 shows the predicted growth of the town and the number of new dwellings needed to meet this increase. Like many of the towns and cities in the South East, Ipswich is partly growing through natural population increase but also through significant inward migration of people. All planning authorities have a duty to plan for a sustainable future. Ipswich Borough Council is no exception and they decided to prioritise the use of **brownfield sites** when planning to meet the housing need. The Waterfront, a large area associated with the old docks and adjacent to the town centre, proved to be ideal for meeting some of the housing need. The location of the Waterfront can be seen on Figure 8.

Figure 7 Population growth of Ipswich and housing need

	Population			Estimated number of new dwellings required
	2001 Census	2021 (predicted)	Change	
Suffolk as a whole	670,200	733,600	+ 63,400	61,700
Ipswich	117,400	138,700	+ 21,300	15,400

The Waterfront vision

The Waterfront is the biggest regeneration project in the East of England. Formerly an industrial dock area with warehouses and factory sites, the site had become increasingly derelict since the 1970s. Ipswich Borough Council, working in partnership with a number of developers, created a vision where new residences would blend with culture, business, and a range of leisure and education opportunities. The best of the old would be retained and striking new designs would show the ambition of the town as it moved into the twenty-first century. Despite the recession throughout 2009, the project is on course to be completed by 2011. The website at www.ipswich.gov.uk (use the search facility within this site) provides you with more detail on each aspect of the scheme.

Figure 8 An Ordnance Survey extract of the location of Ipswich Waterfront. Scale 1:25,000 Sheet 197

Looking west across the new marina towards the high-rise apartments

Re-using the old to create new leisure opportunities amongst the apartments

The few remaining warehouses await development

Figure 9 The vision becomes reality

An A level Geography student undertaking an investigation into the Waterfront interviewed more than 50 residents of the new apartments surrounding the dock and 30 visitors who were enjoying many of the bars and restaurants in the area. From the responses, the development is clearly very popular!

The location is superb. I can walk to my office in the town centre in a matter of minutes and I no longer need to use my car during the week.
I have all the entertainment I need on my doorstep. The bars are lively at night and on a sunny day you can sit and watch the activity in the marina whilst enjoying a latte.
Whilst the rents are not cheap, my apartment has all I need. The small kitchen/diner is fitted out with brand-new appliances and the two bedrooms mean that I can have friends staying over.

This is my first visit to Ipswich. I'm amazed how modern everything looks, but they have done really well to keep some of the old buildings to add character. The four-star hotel I'm staying in was once an old flour mill.
I think they have a really nice balance of places to work, such as the law firms and the estate agents, along with the leisure facilities like the dance studio and the art gallery – and best of all there's a variety of flats and apartments. It would be great to live here. I love the brave architectural styles and colours of the new university buildings. When the halls of residence are completed, this would be a fantastic place to be a student.

Figure 10 The views of residents and visitors

Is it all good news?

With such positive reports, it is difficult to find any opposition to what the planners have achieved in Ipswich. However, one letter, written to the editor of the local newspaper, does voice some concerns …

Dear Sir

Once again your newspaper reports the Waterfront development in a positive way. Was your journalist wearing rose-tinted spectacles when he wrote the feature article in last night's edition of the paper (4 February 2010)? Hasn't he heard that the local council has failed to include enough affordable housing in their plans? I know that the local Labour and Liberal Party are most upset by this oversight. How do you explain that some of the expensive apartments remain empty?

Perhaps the biggest problems have yet to arise. I cannot be alone in thinking that a traffic management scheme for the area has been forgotten. The increase in residents and businesses in the area has choked the already congested road system. I understand that the local roads are now designated as an Air Quality Management Area due to the fumes from stationary cars.

I have no doubt that the council will have to build a new river crossing to ease the traffic flow. To do this it will have to use its powers of compulsory purchase. As always, someone will lose out. They won't think twice about an opportunity to move out one of the few boat repair yards left in the area.

Mr G Dixie,
resident of Ipswich

Figure 11 A letter to the editor …

Activity

1 Study Figure 7. What factors create the need for so many new dwellings in Ipswich?

2 Discuss why the development of sustainable communities needs to include facilities for housing, work and leisure.

3 For a new development close to your school, design a table which has two columns featuring positive and negative aspects of the scheme. Try to consider social, economic and environmental factors when you review the successes and failures of the scheme.

Barcelona

Investigating regeneration – solving one problem, creating another?

Like many other European cities, Barcelona in Spain has experienced rapid growth throughout the twentieth century. The population of the greater metropolitan area has increased from 500,000 in 1930 to over 4 million today.

Activity

1 Study the list of principles used by Barcelona planners set out in Figure 15. Select two from the list and explain why you think the principle is important.

Figure 12 The location of Barcelona

	Population of the metropolitan area	Size of the metropolitan area (Kms²)
1930	500, 000	60
1950	800, 000	125
1970	1,500,000	250
1990	4,000,000	500
2020 (est)	4,200, 000	500

Figure 13 The growth of Barcelona

This rapid growth put tremendous pressure on transport systems and other services in the region. By 1980, 4 per cent of people lived in homes unfit for human habitation and 16 per cent lived in housing areas which lacked basic facilities. Out of this urban chaos Barcelona has now developed a reputation for effective urban regeneration, with cities across Europe copying its methods.

Figure 14 The regeneration of the old coastal industrial area – now called Vila Olimpica

In the 1980s, the planners tackled huge brownfield sites such as the decaying industrial areas adjacent to the port. The 1992 Olympic site was an ideal place for the planners to flex their muscles.

Into the twenty-first century, the move has been away from projects involving the mass clearance of derelict industrial land. Instead the planners are trying to renew and improve existing areas. Figure 15 shows some of the principles that underpin the work of the Barcelona planners.

Figure 15 Planning in Barcelona – how to revive an urban area

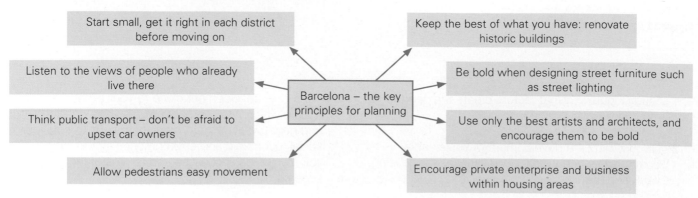

Start small, get it right in each district before moving on

Keep the best of what you have: renovate historic buildings

Listen to the views of people who already live there

Be bold when designing street furniture such as street lighting

Think public transport – don't be afraid to upset car owners

Barcelona – the key principles for planning

Use only the best artists and architects, and encourage them to be bold

Allow pedestrians easy movement

Encourage private enterprise and business within housing areas

One of the first areas to enjoy the benefits of rejuvenation is the El Raval district adjacent to the famous Ramblas in central Barcelona. This was one of the seediest districts of Barcelona with serious problems of crime associated with drugs and prostitution. Today the area is on the up. Apartments have been improved and bars, dancing halls and restaurants have been established. The streetscape has received major investment.

The area had a long history of crime

Today it is vibrant, particularly at night

Figure 16 Rejuvenating the problem district of El Raval

Solve one problem, create another!

Barcelona is now a favourite destination for short breaks. Guide books are crammed with information on how to enjoy the history, art and culture of this exciting city. Some books include an honest assessment of some of the problems you may encounter. In rejuvenated districts like El Raval the vibrant atmosphere at night can be threatening to some visitors and a nightmare for local people who want to catch some sleep.

The city authorities have hit back. In 2006, new by-laws were introduced with on-the-spot fines for:

- noisy revellers, especially in narrow alleys and in streets with balconies
- the inappropriate consumption of alcohol in public places
- graffiti
- the inappropriate use of public areas and street furniture.

Street signs have been posted in problem areas such as El Raval, and buses carry adverts to encourage bikers to move around quietly!

Figure 18 At night thousands of motos are used by young people causing disturbance to residents

Every night the city streets are hosed down, the unpleasant contribution from countless dogs is made worse through drunken humans adding to the stench with rivers of pee. Noise pollution is also a problem in El Raval. The screaming and shouting of revellers combined with the menace of motos leads to sleepless nights for residents. It seems that the youths deliberately alter the muffles on their exhaust system to create maximum noise nuisance. Locals put up signs on balconies demanding quiet. The local authority has started to revoke licences for breaking noise pollution rules.

Damien Simonis – Lonely Planet

Figure 17 Extract from the *Lonely Planet Guide: Barcelona*

Activity

2 In a class discussion, identify areas that suffer from anti-social behaviour. Suggest how the local authority might reduce the problem.

3 The following websites provide you with more information on how Barcelona is leading the way to rejuvenate problem city areas. Study the information and use the links, then list five things that you think British planners should incorporate in their work.
   http://w3.bcn.es
   www.guiabcn.cat/ guiaturistica/en_ordinance. html

What are the current patterns of retailing in European cities?

The pattern of retailing in our large towns and cities is changing rapidly. In some respects, every city and town is unique. Some cities/towns contain shops which reflect local characteristics, for example where tourism is an important function. Some shops reflect the ethnicity of the local population. The range of retail provision is dependent on the size of the city/town and its function (or not), as a regional centre. However, similar patterns of retailing can be seen across all urban areas of the UK.

Most of our towns and cities reflect the same geographical pattern of retail outlets. Consider the map below (Figure 19). How far does it reflect what can be found in your nearest large town or city? What are the similarities, what are the differences?

Fact box 2
- Inner suburban areas feature corner shops. Many have closed down through competition from supermarkets. The remaining shops are open long hours.
- Another characteristic are the parades of shops on feeder roads leading to the CBD.
- Fast-food outlets increasingly dominate, along with shops catering for local ethnic groups.
- Limited parking can be a significant problem, especially on busy commuter routes.

Fact box 3
- Small parades of shops are located in suburban estates.
- Many of the original shops (butcher/greengrocer) have closed through competition from supermarkets.
- Newsagents/off-licences/take-away outlets are a feature.

Fact box 1
- The city/town centre is still an important focus for retail provision.
- There are large covered shopping malls.
- Large department stores are a feature.
- Shopping areas have been pedestrianised.
- Many cities now resemble clone towns. You could be any place, anywhere.
- Streets adjacent to the newly built shopping malls are often in decline, with empty shop units increasingly common. There is an increase in 'pound shops' and charity shops.

Fact box 4
- Large supermarkets have been developed on greenfield sites adjacent to main roads.
- These sites are preferred as they have extensive parking facilities and the main roads allow ease of access for customers and delivery lorries.
- There is often significant local opposition when a new supermarket is proposed.
- Large retail parks have been developed from the 1980s through to the present day.
- Electrical superstores, DIY superstores and furniture warehouses dominate.
- Many retail parks include fast-food outlets.
- Most are open for long hours and include Sunday opening.
- Increasingly, local authorities require brownfield sites to be considered first.

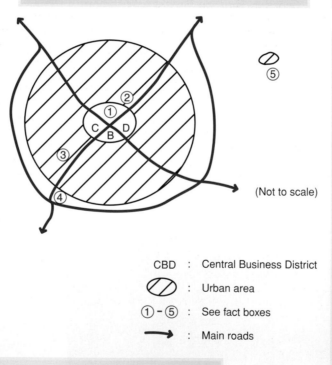

CBD : Central Business District

⬭ : Urban area

①–⑤ : See fact boxes

→ : Main roads

(Not to scale)

Fact box 5
- In small settlements outside the urban area, shopping services have suffered in recent years.
- Often coinciding with the closure of the village post office, village stores cannot compete with supermarkets, which are used by residents whilst commuting to work in the city or town.
- A recent trend has been the growth of farmers' markets at weekends.

Figure 19 The typical pattern of retail provision in UK cities

Different opinions on retail change

Stories like the news headline in Figure 20 are common in our local newspapers. Retail change always creates a range of opinion. Some people are very happy about what is happening in our towns and cities, whilst others are saddened by events. The range of views expressed in Figure 21 show how different people in different circumstances react to the events around them.

New site for superstore meets local opposition

The local planning authority has confirmed that it has over 100 letters of opposition to the proposed supermarket planned for the old cattle market site in East Street. Most opposition is based on the way the supermarket will kill local businesses. We already have enough …

Figure 21 Different views on retail change

Figure 20 News headline about a proposed new site for a superstore

I used to shop locally. All the shopkeepers knew me and I used to chat with them. The butcher and fishmonger closed when they opened the big supermarket a mile away. I can't get to the supermarket easily as I don't drive. Things are a bit cheaper if you buy in bulk. I don't need to, there's only me.

Elderly lady – lives in the suburbs

I was pleased when they opened the new shopping mall in the city centre. It's weatherproof and I can comfortably take my two young girls around with me. There are lifts and toilets and even a roundabout inside the main hall. Parking can be a problem and expensive, but I don't mind as it's just once a week.

Young mother – lives in a village

I must admit I've got mixed feelings about the new retail park on the edge of town. I did find it convenient when I furnished my flat and decorated and upgraded all the kitchen equipment. I have a heavy heart though, as my father ran his own DIY store in the town centre. You could get everything there. Sadly he had to close because of the expensive rates and the competition from the huge superstores.

Professional man – lives in the suburbs

All around us we are saving up problems for the future. We are forcing people into their cars to shop out of town on land that was once green fields. There was nothing wrong with shopping locally. Things may have been more expensive in the corner shops, but they were an important part of the community. The town centre looks increasingly run down. On some streets there is a spiral of decline when key shops move out. It just seems to be banks and building societies mixed with charity shops and pound shops. I hate the shopping malls, they burn electricity day and night, not least for the air conditioning.

Environmentalist – lives in the inner suburbs

Activity

1 Ask your parents what they think about the changes to shopping patterns over the last 30 years. Record their feelings as positive and negative. Share the outcome in class to create a complete list.

2 In addition to the changes already mentioned on these two pages, there are a number of other changes taking place in our lives that have an impact on shopping provision.
   a) Read the information on the right, select one of the changes and suggest how local events/ examples could enable you to gain a greater understanding and awareness of the issue.
   b) Alternatively, after some initial research, suggest up to five websites that would allow students in your class to investigate the issue/change on a national or European scale.

- Post offices are being closed across the country. What is the reason, and how does the closure affect different groups of people?
- People are becoming more aware of 'food miles'. Should we be concerned about the distance some of our food travels before we buy it? What could be done to reduce food miles?
- New sites for superstores/retail parks are always being sought. Local authorities have a duty to promote the use of brownfield sites in the first instance. Why are greenfield sites favoured by store owners?
- Using the internet to shop is becoming increasingly popular. To what extent do your family and friends use it? What are the implications (good and bad) for this trend?

Shrewsbury — Can the town centre fight back?

Figure 22 The historic shopping heart of Shrewsbury

Shrewsbury typifies retail patterns and trends in most UK cities. The traditional shopping area can be found in the historic heart of the town, situated within the great loop of the river Severn. In recent years two shopping malls have been built and some areas in the centre have been pedestrianised. Where Shrewsbury bucks the trend is that it has retained many of the older independent shops, avoiding being labelled a **clone town**. In this section we look at how the local planners, working with partners in retailing, are attempting to re-invigorate the centre. Shops in Shrewsbury were affected by the 2008/09 recession and, as you might expect, there is an ongoing debate within the town about the negative impacts on the town centre of developing suburban retail parks.

Over the last few years, residents of Shrewsbury have voiced their opinions on the increasing number of online forums and weblogs available to them. Shopping provision in the town has been a recurring theme on the forum.

The examples in Figure 24 are typical of the range of views.

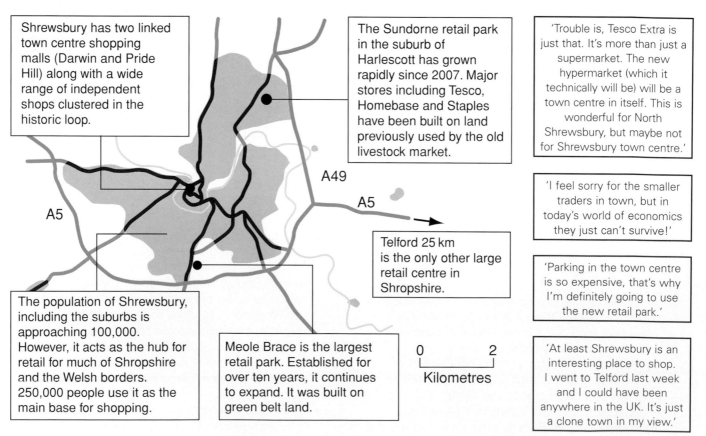

Shrewsbury has two linked town centre shopping malls (Darwin and Pride Hill) along with a wide range of independent shops clustered in the historic loop.

The Sundorne retail park in the suburb of Harlescott has grown rapidly since 2007. Major stores including Tesco, Homebase and Staples have been built on land previously used by the old livestock market.

A49

A5

A5

Telford 25 km is the only other large retail centre in Shropshire.

The population of Shrewsbury, including the suburbs is approaching 100,000. However, it acts as the hub for retail for much of Shropshire and the Welsh borders. 250,000 people use it as the main base for shopping.

Meole Brace is the largest retail park. Established for over ten years, it continues to expand. It was built on green belt land.

0   2
Kilometres

'Trouble is, Tesco Extra is just that. It's more than just a supermarket. The new hypermarket (which it technically will be) will be a town centre in itself. This is wonderful for North Shrewsbury, but maybe not for Shrewsbury town centre.'

'I feel sorry for the smaller traders in town, but in today's world of economics they just can't survive!'

'Parking in the town centre is so expensive, that's why I'm definitely going to use the new retail park.'

'At least Shrewsbury is an interesting place to shop. I went to Telford last week and I could have been anywhere in the UK. It's just a clone town in my view.'

Figure 23 The location of the retail areas in Shrewsbury

Figure 24 Viewpoints of Shrewsbury residents

Can Shrewsbury attract shoppers back to the town centre?

All local authorities face the same issue: they have to meet the needs of the consumers and respond to companies who wish to invest in their towns and cities – hence the development of out-of-town retail parks. On the other hand, the planners don't want to damage the town centre as a vibrant place to visit and shop. The planners in Shrewsbury are working hard to support the smaller independent retailers and the larger stores that wish to remain in the town centre. An initiative that started in Shrewsbury is now being copied across the country. Figure 25 shows how smaller shopkeepers can work together, using modern approaches to retailing. A monthly promotional e-newspaper helps trade and encourages new members to join.

In recent years the planners have worked with shop owners in Shrewsbury. Their aim is to make the town centre a more attractive place in which to shop. Their ideas are wide ranging and efforts will need to continue if Shrewsbury is to fight off competition from the services provided in Telford and beyond. The list below summarises some of the ongoing projects:

- improved town centre signage
- improved parking provision without penalising car owners
- better use of public open space and the promotion of a continental style cafe culture
- more public toilets
- an increase in Sunday trading opportunities
- lower rates to encourage new owners into empty shop units
- joined-up thinking in terms of all infrastructure and services, including public transport.

Figure 25 All The Little Shops scheme

ALL THE LITTLE SHOPS
BUILDING E-FOOTFALL FOR TOWN CENTRES

All The Little Shops/Shrewsbury has been sponsored by *Shropshire Enterprise Partnership and BeVivid* to help the independent retailers of Shrewsbury. Funding has meant all independent retailers and businesses in this region can create their own webpage, display up to 30 products and, if they wish, trade online – totally free.

It is easy for a retailer to set up a shop on this website and just as easy for visitors to the website to see the diverse independent retailers on offer in Shrewsbury, browse a wide range of products, plan their shopping trip, see what else there is to do 'Whilst in Town'.

We hope that All the Little Shops/Shrewsbury will encourage local shopping and increase visits into the shops – but some visitors will be from far away, so we have created a 'secure single payment gateway' which means a visitor can buy a range of products from different shops and pay by credit card – with just one payment.

This important initiative is a first for All the Little Shops – the pilot scheme has been successful and the scheme is now rolling out across the country. It is hoped that by helping local independent retailers – the soul of our town centres in the UK – they will take advantage of this great opportunity and allow the internet to help build awareness of their business and encourage more people into their shops.

Go to: www.allthelittleshops.co.uk for more information

There are good times ahead for town centres across the UK. Rising fuel costs will draw people back into accessible town centres. Out-of-town centres have reached their peak and local authorities will increasingly refuse planning permission under new government legislation. The timeless, ageless appeal of town centres will attract people out of the concrete malls into the social, spiritual and attractive space that historic town centres provide.

Figure 26 Good times ahead?

Activity

1 The news article in Figure 26 is based on the comments made by Sir Stuart Rose, executive of Marks and Spencer, in support of the Shrewsbury town centre forum. How far do you agree with him? Do you support the reasons he gives, that the future for town centres is bright?

2 List five things that you think could be done to re-invigorate town centre shopping areas. Rank the list in order of priority and share the list with your class. Collate the responses and try to rank the top ten ideas.

The rise and rise of internet sales

As well as being hit hard by out-of-town superstores and retail parks, town centre high streets have suffered from the rise and rise of internet shopping. Some of the empty shop units that we see in our high streets can be explained by the closure of shops such as those selling CDs and DVDs. These stores have faced stiff opposition from internet downloads of music and the steady rise of companies such as Amazon, the online book and music sales company.

Figure 27 Zavvi had closed most of its stores by 2009

Figure 28 shows the huge increase in internet use (for shopping) in the period 2001–6.

- UK shoppers spent £3.8 billion online in August 2009, 16 per cent higher than the same month in 2008.
- In total, online sales in the UK were worth £43.8 billion in 2008.
- Online sales at Marks and Spencer rose by 30 per cent in 13 weeks leading up to September 2009.
- John Lewis sales rose by 11.6 per cent to reach £151.5 million for the year up to August 2009.

An interesting fact is that the online shopping revolution has had an impact on different groups of people. The so-called 'silver surfers' – that is, people aged over 65 – are not getting left behind. In fact they accounted for the biggest percentage rise in internet banking users in 2009, with a staggering 275 per cent increase on the previous year. Younger shoppers are embracing the idea too. Advertisers target social networking sites such as Facebook and Twitter, particularly with a view to increasing sales of computer hardware and computer games.

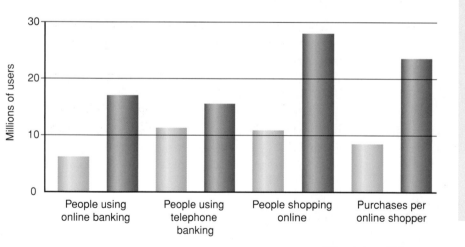

Figure 28 The rise of UK internet shoppers

(chart legend: ▨ 2001 ▨ 2006)

x-axis categories: People using online banking · People using telephone banking · People shopping online · Purchases per online shopper

y-axis: Millions of users (0, 10, 20, 30)

Activity

1 Conduct a survey within your class and at home to find out the online shopping habits in your area. Discuss the questions you need to ask collectively, to enable you to build up a picture of who is buying online and what they are buying.

2 List the positive and negative impacts that the rise and rise of internet shopping is having. Try to think of social, economic and environmental impacts.

Silver surfer

Since I bought a computer, I haven't looked back. I love shopping online. I don't have transport and I'm a bit frail now. It saves me the worry and hassle of having to go to the shops as everything is delivered to my door. Things are a bit cheaper online as well – that's important if you only get a pension. When my local post office closed I decided to get my pension paid straight into my online bank account.

Dell have been delighted by the advertising campaign launched through Twitter. In 2008/9 we have generated sales of over £1.8 million, with people clicking directly from 'tweets'.

Spokesperson for Dell

Figure 29 All ages are embracing the internet sales revolution

Swansea — Amazon locates new warehouse in Swansea

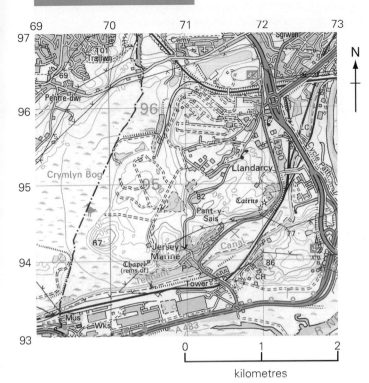

Figure 30 An Ordnance Survey extract showing the location of the Amazon warehouse. Scale 1:50,000 Sheet 170. The centre of the warehouse is at 711934

Figure 31 The huge Amazon warehouse near Swansea

Amazon is one of the leading online retailers in the UK. In 2008 it opened its fourth distribution warehouse in the UK. Situated at Jersey Marine to the east of Swansea, it occupies land where the former Delta Compton aluminium works was once located (see Figure 30). Other UK warehouse locations include Glenrothes in Fife, Gourock in Inverclyde, and Milton Keynes, Buckinghamshire. The site at Swansea employs 1,200 full-time workers and covers a land area equivalent to 10 football pitches.

When the warehouse was opened in 2008, it received positive support from most people, but there were a few negative comments. Look at the range of views expressed below:

- 'This is a powerful shot in the arm for the Welsh economy. It's about jobs for the future.'
- 'The construction jobs alone will create jobs for years.'
- 'It's not just warehouse workers and delivery drivers. There will be jobs for management and jobs in IT support.'
- 'The new link road to the M4 motorway will improve road links for all the other industries nearby.'
- 'To have such a big name in e-commerce will put the region on the map – it's bound to attract other industries.'

- 'We're losing manufacturing jobs and becoming a nation of service workers; this can't be good in the long run.'
- 'Most of the jobs will be low pay – that's hardly a boost for the economy.'
- 'It's places like this that are killing our high street. It's not going to help us regenerate the city centre shopping area of Swansea.'

Activity

3 Look at Figures 30 and 31. Suggest why this is an ideal site for the warehouse.

4 Use a map of the UK and locate all of the Amazon warehouses. Describe the distribution of the warehouses and suggest reasons why Amazon selected these sites.

5 Consider the views on the opening of the new warehouse. In your class, debate if this factory and the rise of internet shopping as a whole, is largely good for the UK.

Organising your own enquiry

When Theme 11 is used as the context for controlled assessment tasks, the topic can generate a wealth of information.

Creating effective questionnaires

Questionnaires are an ideal way to collect data on differing views about retail change. To help you, imagine that a student has been asked to carry out an investigation into the decline of retailing in town centres. If you are asked to devise your own questionnaire, make sure that you consider the following before you start:

- What questions should you ask that will be of *direct relevance* to the investigation?
- How can you shape the individual questions to make the data generated easy to understand and easy to turn into visual/graphical material?
- How many questions do you ask and how many people do you need to ask?

Too many questionnaires contain questions that complicate the research unnecessarily. Keep the questions directly relevant to your investigation.

✗ Don't ask introductory questions that will never be used in the analysis, e.g. *How old are you?; Where do you live?*

✓ Do ask questions directly related to the overall theme, such as questions related to how frequently people shop in the town centre; if they can give any evidence of decline in town centres; if they can suggest reasons why town centres might be struggling to keep customers; if they have experience of using alternative locations for their shopping; why they might prefer the alternative locations.

✗ Don't ask open-ended questions as the responses are too difficult to record.

✓ Use closed questions. The responses are easy to record at the time and, when you come to graph and analyse the results, they make your life so much easier. There are many ways to ask closed questions – two examples are given here:

Example 1

Do you think that the town centre shopping area has declined in the last ten years? Please tick one of the boxes on this 5-point scale:

No I think that the town centre shops are as good today as they have always been.

1 2 3 4 5
☐ ☐ ☐ ☐ ☐

Yes the area has declined significantly in recent years.

Example 2

Many people prefer to shop in out-of-town supermarkets or on retail parks. Please look at the list below. In your opinion, select the five main reasons why you think people might prefer out-of-town shopping to town centre shopping.

Shops are open longer hours ☐

Parking is free ☐

Prices are cheaper ☐

Roads are less congested ☐

The shops are less congested ☐

You can get everything in one place ☐

There are no stairs to climb ☐

The environment is less hectic ☐

✓ Share the same questionnaire with students in your class. You will collect more data (try to ask at least 50 people). The more people you ask, the more reliable your results will be.

Using secondary data from the internet

Many students make the mistake of just cutting and pasting information into their assignment – job done. I'm afraid not! You will only gain credit if you *use* the secondary data and relate it to your enquiry. There are several ways to do this, including:

- highlighting key words/phrases within the article and then discussing why you have drawn attention to them

- cutting photographs/maps from the article and annotating what they show in relation to your investigation

- lifting information from the article and putting it into a table to present evidence to support your findings, or evidence that contradicts your findings

Always acknowledge the source of the data by naming the website, giving the full url address.

GIS Activity: Barcelona city council website

http://w20.bcn.cat:1100/GuiaMap

Barcelona is a large city in Catalonia on the North East coast of Spain. The city council has an excellent GIS on its website. You can view a map of the whole city, as in Figure 32, or use the zoom function to view individual streets in great detail.

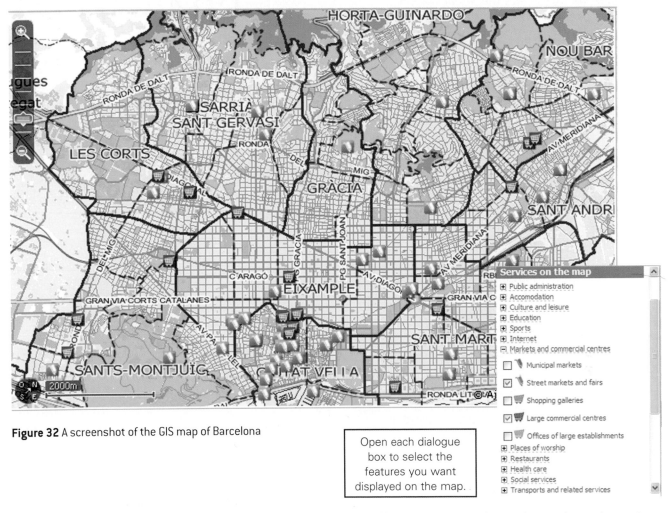

Figure 32 A screenshot of the GIS map of Barcelona

Open each dialogue box to select the features you want displayed on the map.

Figure 33 A screenshot showing you how to choose the services you want to display on the map

Activity

1 a) Describe the distribution of large commercial centres.
b) Suggest why so many are on major roads such as Av. Diagonal.

2 a) Compare the distribution of these larger centres to the street markets and fairs.
b) Give reasons for the differences you have noticed.

How do changes in European consumer choice have a global impact?

What are the impacts of increased consumer choice?

In this section we investigate the impact of UK consumers on people across the world and on the environment. You will see that the spending power of UK consumers has a far-reaching impact on people and places. Some impacts are positive whilst others are negative. One thing is certain, people who live in the UK have enormous spending power. Despite the temporary nature of the recession in 2008/9, the UK remains one of the richest countries in the world. The information in Figure 34 provides evidence of this fact.

Activity

1 The figures given for GDP (PPP) are taken from the *CIA World Factbook*. Find out more by looking at https://www.cia.gov/library/publications/the-world-factbook/rankorder/2001rank.html

2 Find out what is meant by *disposable income*. Why is it an important measure to show the potential spending power of consumers?

clothing and footwear £47,507
food and non-alcoholic beverages £84,993

education £14,100

health £13,659

alcoholic beverages and tobacco £31,120

Figure 34 The spending power of UK consumers in millions

Rank position	Country	GDP (PPP, $ millions)
2	USA	14,260,000
8	UK	2,226,000
13	Spain	1,403,000
59	Morocco	136,600
163	Sierra Leone	4,285

Source: *CIA World Factbook* (2008)

3 Looking at this information as a whole, how far does it confirm that the spending power of UK consumers is likely to have a major impact on people across the world and on environments?

What is the global reach of the UK consumer?

Figure 35 shows a small selection of consumer products purchased in the UK. The source of each product is shown. It is clear that the UK consumer enjoys buying the best from across the world.

Activity

4 Carry out a survey in your home. Find out the source of ten products purchased from around the world. Include at least two examples from each of the three categories of food, clothing and electrical products. Share the information when you are in class and plot the source countries on a world map. Use an atlas to find the location of the source country. Try to add detail by colour-coding the arrows to show different product types.

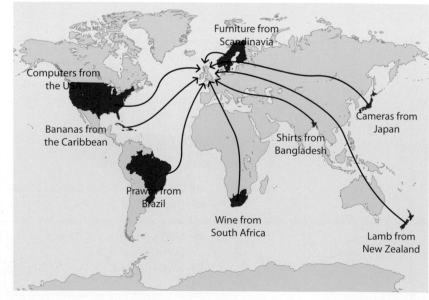

Figure 35 The source of selected products purchased in the UK

Positive impacts of UK consumer spending

In 2009 it is estimated that more than 135,000 Kenyans were employed in growing and packaging flowers for the UK market. Figure 37 illustrates the positive multiplier impact that this employment brings.

Figure 36 Kenyan roses for the UK consumer

Figure 37 The positive multiplier effect of jobs created in Kenya

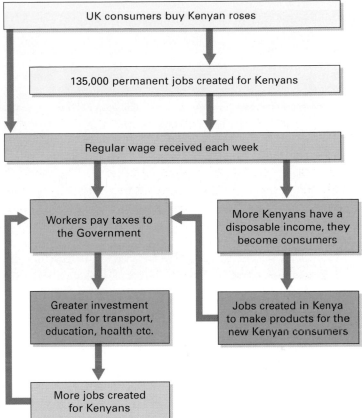

Is it all good news?

The answer is a definite NO! Our desire for world-sourced products, has far-reaching and sometimes surprising effects. Figure 38 illustrates a small selection of the wide-ranging negative impacts that can stem from consumer spending in countries like the UK. Consumerism creates social, economic and environmental problems.

Prawns caught in Scottish waters are shipped across the world to Asia for processing and then back again to the UK. The carbon footprint and associated high 'food miles' generated by this is made worse by the fact that the product needs to be frozen throughout its journey. Find out more at: http://news.bbc.co.uk/1/hi/uk/7150834.stm or use search words 'Scampi and food miles'.

In addition to the debate about smoking, high consumer demand for tobacco has created a number of problems. Land, originally used for food production across the developing world, is being taken out of production as farmers are lured into growing tobacco for profit. Natural forest is being destroyed to create new plantations. Find out more at: www.quitbecause.org.uk/environment.php#tobaccoanddeforest or use search words 'Land loss through tobacco'.

Cotton is used in the clothes industry. It is estimated (2009) that the world trade in cotton is over $32 billion. A lot of production takes place in LEDCs. This trade should bring wealth and prosperity to the producing countries but to meet the demand of the consumer nations, at a price that suits them, there are tales of child labour and the over-use of pesticides. Find out more at: www.ejfoundation.org/page327.html or use search words 'Child labour and environmental problems with cotton'.

Every day the UK creates enough waste to fill the Royal Albert Hall in London. Despite attempts to recycle, our throwaway consumer society is filling up all available landfill sites and is pushing local authorities towards the use of controversial incinerator plants. Find out more at: www.guardian.co.uk/environment/2007/jan/19/waste or use the search words 'Running out of landfill'.

Figure 38 Some of the negative impacts of consumer spending

Ethical consumers and the fashion trade

Figure 39 Factory conditions in Asia

Most people are keen to enjoy affordable, fashionable clothes from the UK high street stores. Most consumers agree that production workers in Asia should receive a fair day's pay whilst working in a safe environment.

In 2008, an investigation by the BBC into Primark accused the leading high street fashion retailer of:

- breaking its ethical trading policy and ignoring its social responsibility guarantee
- allowing child labour to produce many of its fashion items
- allowing workers to work in unregulated sweatshop conditions.

Extracts of a company statement issued shortly after the BBC broadcast its programme can be seen in Figure 40.

Two years earlier the charity War on Want produced a report 'Fashion Victims: The True Cost of Cheap Clothes', in which it highlighted the plight of Asian workers trying to live on poverty wages whilst working in sweatshop conditions. The report suggested that workers in Asia live in terrible poverty to allow us to buy fashionable clothes at cheap prices. Today the same charity reports that little has changed.

Panorama – right of reply

'Production of the garments identified by the BBC was sub-contracted without Primark's knowledge or consent.

We acted immediately by cancelling all new orders with them and withdrawing items from sale.

Under our Code of Conduct, children are expressly forbidden to work on clothes produced for us.

Primark supports some 2 million people through its supply contracts. As part of its contribution, the company has already announced its intention to establish the 'Primark Better Lives Foundation', which will provide financial assistance to organizations devoted to improving the lives of young people.'

Figure 40 Extracts from the Primark statement, June 2008

www.waronwant.org/campaigns/ supermarkets-and-sweatshops/fashion-victims
A full copy of the report can be found at this address. Also search 'War on Want campaigns' for the latest information.

FIGHTING GLOBAL POVERTY

Figure 41 War on Want

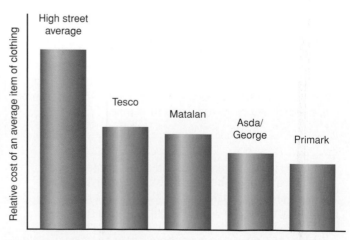

Figure 42 The relative cost of clothes, as shown in the War on Want report. Source: 'Primark Kings of Budget Clothing', *Daily Record*, 3 December 2005

In a geography lesson at her Bristol College, A Level student Claire talked about her mixed feelings after studying the issues raised by the report. You can see from her comments in Figure 43 that it is not always easy to reach conclusions over such controversial issues.

> On the one hand I appreciate that lots of jobs are created in Asia, not least in the rural areas where full-time, paid work is difficult to come by. I understand that lots of NGOs oversee the working conditions to make sure that people are treated fairly and with respect.

> On the other hand, there are many stories on the news that make me think long and hard about whether I should shop for cheaper fashion products. Some of the students from my college decided to disrupt the opening of the new Primark store in Bristol last week.

Figure 43 Difficult to reach conclusions

Whatever the arguments, on both sides of the issue, UK consumers (not least the younger consumers) continue to shop at the cheaper high street fashion stores. Throughout 2009 and into 2010, the media was full of stories on how chains like George, Primark, Tesco and Matalan go from strength to strength, even at a time of recession.

News Report

March 2010

High street fashion stores, catering for the cheaper end of the market go from strength to strength, even through the recession. One chain, Primark, reported a year on year increase of 21 per cent on sales.

The success of the chain is based on holding down prices and giving value for money. At a time when the high street is being hit hard, as seen by the number of vacant shop units in our town centres, Primark opened 11 new stores in 2009 and now has 190 throughout the UK. New outlets in Portugal and Germany are planned.

Figure 45 Profits soar

Figure 44 Protests outside the new Primark store in Bristol, August 2009

Figure 46 Bargain hunters flock to the new Primark store

Activity

1   This issue is complex and very controversial. There is a wealth of information available to help you develop your thinking. Carry out research on the internet. Use search terms such as 'ethical shopper' or 'ethical consumer'.

Merthyr Tydfil — What is the impact of our consumer society on the environment?

The disposal of household waste is a messy and controversial issue. There are wide-ranging views and heated arguments taking place all over the UK, not least when news breaks that a named area is the favoured location for a new landfill or incinerator site. In this case study we look at the background to the issue and then focus on the hugely controversial debate surrounding an incinerator for Merthyr Tydfil, Wales.

Did you know ...?

- Every year each UK household produces over 1 tonne of rubbish.
- Every person in the UK throws away their own body weight in rubbish every seven weeks.
- In recent years, local and national governments have spent millions of pounds persuading consumers and producers to reduce packaging and recycle waste. The many initiatives that exist have had some effect but as a country we still lag behind our European neighbours. In 1997 we recycled just 7 per cent of our waste, now it is almost up to 27 per cent. The Netherlands and Germany recycle around 50 per cent of their waste.

- Landfills have been the most common way to dispose of waste in the UK. There are many advantages of using this method: it is relatively cheap; lots of different waste can be disposed of without the cost of sorting; the gasses given off can be used for heating; the waste remains in the UK and doesn't become a burden for less developed countries. However there are increasingly few new sites available as old sites become full.
- As available landfill sites are used up and recycling continues to gather pace, but only slowly, local authorities are increasingly turning to incinerators to dispose of waste. There are advantages such as: electricity can be generated in the process; the bulk of waste is reduced by as much as 95 per cent; they are increasingly cost effective compared with landfill; they are a good business opportunity for international companies. However, the use of incinerators attracts significant opposition: voters who live near proposed sites will probably be strongly against the idea; greenhouse gas emissions are significant; at some sites, there have been rumours of noxious gas emissions such as dioxins; the introduction of incinerators detracts from local recycling initiatives.

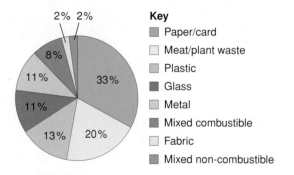

Key
- Paper/card
- Meat/plant waste
- Plastic
- Glass
- Metal
- Mixed combustible
- Fabric
- Mixed non-combustible

Figure 47 What is household waste made up of?

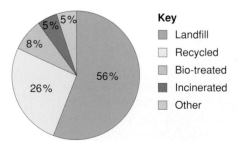

Key
- Landfill
- Recycled
- Bio-treated
- Incinerated
- Other

Figure 48 Where does UK waste go?

recycle for Wales
ailgylchu dros Gymru
www.wasteawarenesswales.org.uk

Figure 49 Recycle for Wales logo

Find out more about recycling by visiting these websites.
www.recycling-guide.org.uk
www.recycle-more.co.uk
www.defra.gov.uk/environment/waste/index.htm
www.wasteawarenesswales.org.uk
www.craffamwastraff.org.uk/index.html (Welsh language version)

Incinerator planned for Merthyr?

In 2009 news broke through the 'Wales Online' news service (www.walesonline.co.uk) that Merthyr Tydfil was the site chosen for an incinerator. Figure 50 presents the mixed views on the project from the outset.

£400m giant waste incinerator bid for Ffos-y-fran

5 February 2009 by Jackie Bow, Merthyr Express

PLANS for a massive £400m energy-producing waste incinerator next to the controversial Ffos-y-fran opencast site have been revealed. The new facility, known as Brig-y-Cwm, would create up to 600 jobs, 500 during construction and 100 full-time jobs when operating.

The incinerator's backers American owners Covanta Energy, the Welsh Assembly Government and International Business Wales, expect the plant to generate about 70 megawatts of electricity – enough to supply power to up to 180,000 homes from around 750,000 tonnes of waste.

The proposed site on land at Cwmbargoed, borders Merthyr Tydfil and Caerphilly. Environmentalists and residents living near the proposed site greeted the news with dismay.

Malcolm Chilton, Covanta Energy's UK managing director, said: 'We supply millions of homes with clean energy from non-recyclable waste, and we pledge to consult with local people in the months ahead to seek views and suggestions on our proposal for Merthyr Tydfil.'

If it gets the go-ahead the plant, financed and operated by Covanta, will be operational by 2013–14. The waste would arrive by rail in sealed containers from various locations across Wales. There would be less need for local authorities to use landfill sites, cutting costs, and it could mean cheaper electricity for people in neighbouring communities.

Council leader Jeff Edwards said he had not been involved in any negotiations. He believes it is: 'A very positive project and a huge opportunity for Merthyr Tydfil' with job creation, reduced electricity charges, and savings for the Council on landfill. 'I know one of the concerns raised was the emission from the plant. It will not include dioxins and will meet American emission standards, which are far higher than European and UK standards.'

Terry Evans, chairman of Residents against Ffos-y-fran says it is another blow for the area. 'We've got Ffos-y-fran, Trecatti landfill site, there's a decision pending on a prison nearby and now this,' he said. 'Merthyr has become a dumping ground. What next will be foisted on us?'

Haf Elgar, a Friends of the Earth campaigner, warned that the proposed plant would probably take all the waste from Wales and parts of England and bring it to South Wales. She said: 'A plant of that size would probably take more residual waste than is produced in Wales. It completely goes against the proximity principle of dealing with waste locally and would mean even more pollution for residents of the Merthyr area.'

Figure 50 A newspaper article on a proposed incinerator in Merthyr Tydfil

Activity

1   Read Figure 50. What do you think about the proposal to construct an incinerator near Merthyr?

2   There is a lot of information on the web to help you with more detailed research. Use basic search words such as 'Incinerator planned for Ffos-y-fran' or go to specific websites. Many of these have been set up to oppose the site, so remember that you may only get one side of the story. Try the websites at:
    http://covantaenergy.co.uk/site/wales (includes YouTube video produced by Covanta)
    www.stopffosyfran.co.uk/Incinerator.html (includes YouTube video clips on related matters)
    http://news.bbc.co.uk/1/hi/wales/south_east/7933320.stm

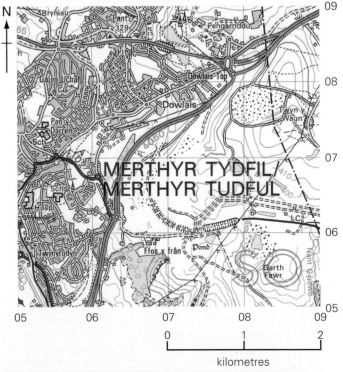

Figure 51 An Ordance Survey extract of the location of the proposed incinerator south-east of Merthyr. Scale 1:50,000 Sheet 160

Understanding maps

Maps are an essential tool for geographers and examiners are keen to find out if you can read, understand, interpret and use the information that a map holds. You may also be invited to draw a sketch map. It is almost certain that in your GCSE examination at least one question will contain an Ordnance Survey map, and it is likely that other questions will contain choropleth, statistical or sketch maps.

It is therefore vital that you are able to:

- read symbols, give grid references and directions, measure distances and understand contour lines
- describe and explain geographical features shown on a map e.g. physical features such as hills and river valleys or human features such as settlement patterns and locations
- draw a clear and labelled sketch map
- use the information that a map provides, along with your own geographical knowledge, in a decision-making exercise.

Sample question

Study Figure 31 on page 101. With the help of a labelled sketch map explain the location of the Amazon warehouse near Swansea.

Student answer

Title – The location of the Amazon warehouse

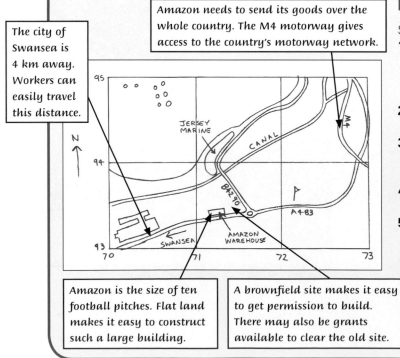

The city of Swansea is 4 km away. Workers can easily travel this distance.

Amazon needs to send its goods over the whole country. The M4 motorway gives access to the country's motorway network.

Amazon is the size of ten football pitches. Flat land makes it easy to construct such a large building.

A brownfield site makes it easy to get permission to build. There may also be grants available to clear the old site.

Drawing a sketch map

Sketch maps have many uses. In your controlled assessment you may draw a sketch map to outline the area of your study. In an examination you may decide to include a sketch map in your answer to exemplify the points you are making e.g. of a tourist region that you have studied (this would impress an examiner and in a levels question would help you achieve a level 3 answer). You may also be asked to draw a sketch map, or add detail to one which has been partly drawn, to test your mapping skills.

The first step in completing a good sketch map is to draw a simple outline. If you are sketching an OS map it is a good idea to copy the grid from the map onto your paper to give a frame for your drawing. Add information such as names of towns, roads and rivers. Give your map a title, scale and a north sign and always draw in pencil. Use annotation to answer the question that you have been set. Look at how much time you have, and how many marks a question is worth, this will guide the amount of detail you need to add.

What the examiner has to say!

This is a very good quality fieldsketch. It is neat, clear, detailed and the annotation is relevant and detailed. The only significant omission is the lack of a scale. Shading could have also been used to mark areas of higher land.

Exam practice

Study Figure 51 on page 109.

1. Give the six figure grid reference for:
   a) Isaac Morgan Cottages
   b) the roundabout where the A4102 meets the A4060T.
2. Which two ways of showing height above sea level can be seen in grid square 0706?
3. Describe the shape of the land around the proposed site for the waste incinerator at Ffros-y-fran.
4. Give two pieces of map evidence to suggest this area was once an important mining area.
5. With the help of a labelled sketch map describe the location for the proposed waste incinerator at Ffros-y-fran. Annotate your sketch map to suggest why this may be a good location for such a development.

What are the current patterns of employment in Wales?

GO Wales is a website where you can apply for work experience in Wales. The website also highlights graduate job opportunities in the following organisations:

- Four of the world's six main high-tech electronics, aerospace, engineering and telecommunications companies are based in Wales: BT, Vodaphone, T-Mobile and NTL have bases and call centres.
- Fibre-optic technology is prospering in Wales, employing over 30 per cent of the UK's workforce in this sector.
- Biotechnology companies are expanding, with 70 health-care companies employing over 13,000 staff.
- Wales has some of the best media output in the UK, including print and broadcast, film and television, music and entertainment.
- Seven of the UK's top ten food processors have operations here, including multi-nationals, Unilever and Kellogg's.

Figure 1 GO Wales

In Snowdonia, the majority of people are employed in the primary and tertiary sectors (farming and quarrying, tourism).

Swansea and Cardiff have the highest employment in the tertiary sectors (both 87 per cent).

Flintshire has the highest employment in production and construction (38 per cent).

Figure 2 Different jobs in contrasting areas of Wales

How do we classify work and employment?

The usual way to classify employment is to sort all economic activities into one of three sectors:

- **Primary sector** – this sector produces raw materials such as a food crop, timber or a mineral. Jobs in fishing, mining and quarrying are examples of primary economic occupations.
- **Secondary sector** – this sector is involved in processing and manufacturing. Food processing and the manufacture of microchips or aircraft wings are examples of secondary economic occupations.
- **Tertiary sector** – this sector provides services to other industries or to individual people like you and me. Employment in a school, hospital or hotel are examples of tertiary economic occupations.

A recent development in the way we record employment is to identify jobs in the **knowledge economy**. These jobs require high levels of training or education. They include jobs in:

- **high-tech industries**, such as defence systems, medical equipment
- **medium/high-tech industries**, such as electronics
- **knowledge-intensive industries**, such as finance, Technium (support from a local university to people setting up their own business).

Public and private sectors

Employment can be either in the public or the private sector.

- People working in the **public sector** are employed by the national, regional or local government. This includes teachers, nurses, social workers, planners and soldiers.
- People working in the **private sector** are either self-employed or work for a company not owned by the government. The private sector provides a wide range of jobs on the land (farming, forestry), in construction (design, engineering, building), and in manufacturing and services (car assembly, building turbines for wind farms).

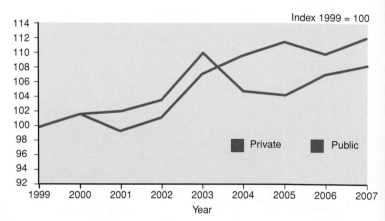

Figure 4 Changing employment in Wales by public/private sector. To make comparison easier, the number of people employed in each sector in 1999 has been converted to an index of 100

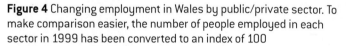

	Public sector	Private sector
Male	36.3	61.7
Female	63.7	38.3

Figure 5 Percentage employment, public and private sectors in Wales by gender, 2007

	Numbers in thousands
Agriculture, hunting, forestry and fishing	38
Mining and quarrying	2
Manufacturing	167
Energy and water	6
Construction	100
Distribution (retail, wholesale, motor trades and repairs)	215
Hotels and restaurants	92
Transport, storage and communication	61
Finance and business activities	191
Public administration	93
Education	123
Health	184
Other industries	82
All industries	**1354**
All production (secondary) industries	**271**
All service (tertiary) industries	**1029**

Figure 3 Workplace employment by industry, Wales 2007

What are the current geographical patterns of work within Wales?

The number of people working in the primary, secondary and tertiary sectors is known as the **employment structure** of that region. Different regions of Wales have different employment structures. So what is the geographical pattern of jobs in Wales?

In Figure 6, the vertical line represents the fact that 59 per cent of all jobs are in West Wales and the Valleys. Where the bars are far from this vertical line it shows that these jobs are over- or under-represented.

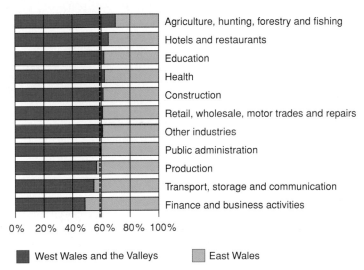

Agriculture, hunting, forestry and fishing
Hotels and restaurants
Education
Health
Construction
Retail, wholesale, motor trades and repairs
Other industries
Public administration
Production
Transport, storage and communication
Finance and business activities

0%   20%   40%   60%   80%   100%

■ West Wales and the Valleys   ■ East Wales

Figure 6 Employment in Wales, 2007

What is the pattern of farming in Wales?

Eighty per cent of Wales has been classified by the European Union as a **Less Favoured Area (LFA)**. This area is difficult to farm due to the glaciated mountainous landscape which has steep slopes and thin soils. The climate of this area is unsuitable for many crops. There are few fast road or rail connections to large populations which provide markets for fresh food. The dominant farming type in such marginal land is livestock. Ninety per cent of Welsh sheep farming is found in the LFA. Dairying is more dominant in West Wales, with beef cattle more common in Powys. Farms in coastal areas grow more crops. The main cereal crop is barley. Farms in the warmer, lower coastal areas nearer the larger towns grow vegetables.

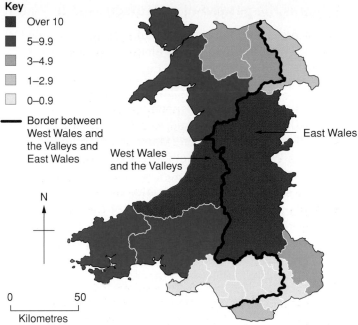

Key
■ Over 10
■ 5–9.9
■ 3–4.9
□ 1–2.9
□ 0–0.9
— Border between West Wales and the Valleys and East Wales

East Wales
West Wales and the Valleys

N

0   50
Kilometres

Figure 7 Percentage of people employed in farming in each authority of Wales

Activity

1 Classify the types of graduate job included on the GO Wales website (Figure 1).

2 Study Figure 3.
   a) Which were the four most important employers in the tertiary sector?
   b) Which were the two most important employers in the public sector?
   c) What percentage was employed in the:
      i) tertiary ii) secondary iii) primary sectors?

3 Use Figure 4 to describe what has happened to private sector jobs since 1999.

4 Use Figures 4 and 5 to describe the main differences between public and private sector jobs.

5 Suggest reasons for the differences in employment shown in Figure 6 in East and West Wales.

6 Use Figure 7 and the text to describe the distribution of farming jobs in Wales.

What is the pattern of manufacturing in Wales?

There are many high-tech manufacturing firms in Wales which are involved in electronics, aerospace, and medicines. However, as Figures 8 and 9 show, these firms are not evenly distributed.

In 2008, the Welsh aerospace industry employed 25,000 people who worked in 180 companies with annual sales of £3 billion. Many aeroplane parts are made in Wales. These include the huge plane wings, made at Airbus in Broughton, which need an open factory space equivalent to twelve full-size football pitches. After assembly, the wings of the Airbus are transported one by one by road and then down the River Dee to Mostyn Harbour, where they are loaded onto the specially built roll-on/roll-off ferry which takes them to Toulouse in France.

www.aerospacewalesforum.com
This website provides news and information for industries involved in the aerospace industries in Wales. Click on the interactive map to discover more about each of its members.

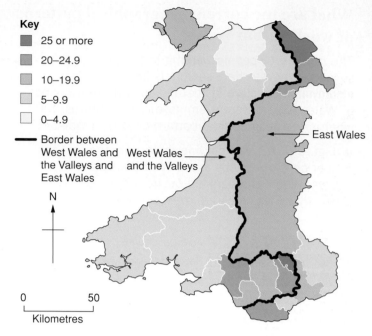

Figure 8 Percentage of people employed in production (manufacturing, energy and water) in each authority of Wales

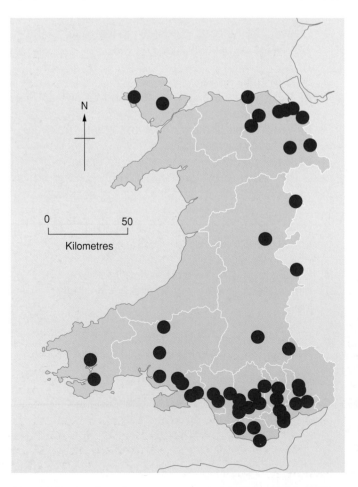

Figure 9 The location of some aerospace industries in Wales, 2009

Activity

1 Study Figure 8. Describe the distribution of authorities that have more than 20 per cent of the workforce employed in manufacturing.

2 Study Figure 9. Describe the distribution of aerospace companies across Wales.

3 a) Make a table, Aerospace Wales, with four columns using the following headings:

   Manufacture of aeroplane parts

   Maintenance, repair, overhaul (MRO)

   Research and Development of new ideas

   Training, development of skills

   b) Go to the interactive map on Aerospace Wales' website:
   www.aerospacewalesforum.com/home. php?page_id=37
   and click on a selection of the pins. For each location insert a summary of the industry in the appropriate column.

Using resources

In your examination you will be given information in the form of OS maps, data, diagrams, graphs, newspaper articles and perhaps cartoons. Examiners often use one of these resources as a starting point for a question. It is important that you study resources carefully: often the answer to a question can be found in the information given or you may be able to use examples in the resources to support your answer. Top tips:

- Read the title carefully and understand the purpose of the resource.
- Highlight what may be important information in the resource, after reading the question.
- Study the key of any map or diagram and look at the axes of graphs.
- Make sure you understand what a graph is showing.
- Look for patterns and trends in the resource.
- Identify any information and data that does not fit (anomalies).

Sample questions

1 Study Figure 4 on page 112.
   (i) Describe the trend in the number of people working in the public sector. [4]
   (ii) Compare the number of people working in the public and private sectors. [4]
2 Study Figure 8 on page 114.
   Describe the distribution pattern of employment in production across Wales. [4]

Student answer

1 (i) In 1999 there was a starting index of 100. There was a steady rise✓ in the number of people reaching a peak of 110 in 2003.✓ There was a sharp decrease to 105 in 2004✓ and then yo-yoes up until 2007.
(ii) Both sectors started out in 1999 with an index of 100. As the public sector increased the private sector decreased✓ until 2002. Both sectors rose✓ in 2003 but then the private continued to rise whereas the public fell✓ until 2005. After 2005 both sectors rose✓ although the private sector had a higher finishing index of 111 compared to✓ the public sector of 108.

Student answer

2 There is more production industry in the east than in the west.✓ The main areas of employment are South Wales and North East.✓

Patterns and trends

To describe a pattern is to describe how similar features are spread across a map. For example the settlement pattern of a region may be described as dispersed, nucleated or linear. Trends are patterns on a graph that show how something is changing over time.

Comparing information

Compare asks you to think in a comparative manner and not to simply write two separate descriptions. You need to say how patterns and trends are similar and different, using phrases such as 'compared with, 'whereas', 'on the other hand' and 'although'.

What the examiner has to say!

(i) This is a good answer. The candidate has described the trend from 1999 to 2003 and quantified the rise. The candidate notes the decline in 2003 and 2004 but fails to score full marks by describing the trend as 'yo-yoing' whereas there was a small decrease to 2005 and then a significant increase into 2007 to a final index of 108. This answer scores 3 marks.

(ii) A very good answer. It is not accurate to state that the private sector decreased until 2002. However, the candidate recognises that the public sector rises compared with the private sector and for this I would award a mark. The candidate continues to make four clear points easily achieving the maximum mark of 4.

What the examiner has to say!

This is a disappointing answer. The candidate has clear understanding of the demands of the question but distribution patterns are described in very general terms. South Wales and north-east Wales are very large areas; more specific detail was needed to clearly describe the pattern. The candidate could also have gained further marks by quantifying descriptions.

What is the future of employment in Wales?

How and why are patterns of work changing?

Technology is having a massive impact on all sectors of the economy. **Mechanisation**, the use of machines to replace human labour, has been a major cause of job losses, especially in the primary and manufacturing sectors. At the same time, new computer and communication technology is creating new jobs in some service industries.

Another change is the globalisation of industry. Many firms in Wales are **multi-national companies (MNCs)**. They may have headquarters in Asia or elsewhere in Europe. MNCs need to make a profit. They may close factories in Wales if they think that they can make their product cheaper elsewhere. They tend to protect decision-making and research jobs, and these are usually located in the home nation, not abroad.

Area of employment	% Change: 2001 to 2006
Agriculture, hunting, forestry and fishing	+1%
Mining and quarrying	-38%
Manufacturing	-18%
Energy and water	-29%
Construction	+24%
Distribution (retail, wholesale, motor trades and repair)	+1%
Hotels and restaurants	+9%
Transport, storage and communication	-1%
Finance and business activities	+28%
Public administration	+14%
Education	+7%
Health	+11%
Other industries	+21%
All industries	**+7%**
All production	**-18%**
All service industries	**+11%**

Figure 10 Changes in employment in Wales, 2001 to 2006

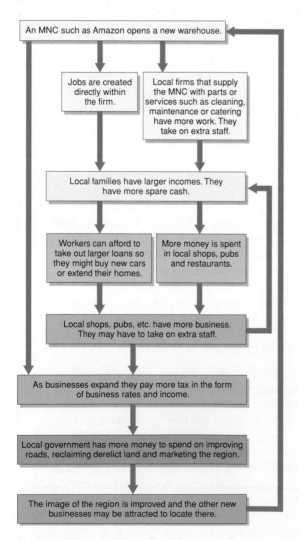

Figure 11 The positive multiplier effect

Neath Port Talbot — The growth of internet retailing

Some of the world's fastest-growing businesses are associated with the expansion of business on the internet. Amazon is an American-owned internet retail company. It opened its fourth and largest distribution centre (ten football pitches in size) in the UK – Neath Port Talbot, Swansea Bay – in 2008 (see page 101). This centre supplies books, home and garden products, jewellery, sporting goods and electronics to 200 countries.

Amazon chose this location because there was:

- a large, flat plot of land available with planning permission
- a new access road built by Neath Port Talbot Council
- an attractive local environment (Gower)
- a grant from the Welsh Assembly Government (WAG).

When an MNC such as Amazon opens a new factory or office it can have a positive impact on local people and the local economy. Some jobs are created by the firm itself: The new warehouse in Swansea Bay created 1,200 full-time and 1,500 seasonal jobs. This is a direct benefit of the investment made by Amazon in the UK. These new jobs may help to stimulate extra work for other local businesses. This extra work is an indirect benefit of the investment made by the MNC. These benefits to the local economy are known as a **positive multiplier effect**.

Figure 12 Amazon's distribution centre

Amazon will bring good wages and prospects to the area from a reputable, expanding company.

A Neath Port Talbot spokesperson

There is concern at the replacement of manufacturing jobs with insecure, low-paid employment in the service sector. These jobs do not provide the foundations for young people to play a full role within their communities.

Figure 13 Different views of the development   **The union, Unite**

Activity

1 **a)** Choose and use a suitable technique to represent the data in Figure 10.
   b) Describe the changes of employment in Wales between 2001 and 2006.

2 Draw an annotated sketch of the location of the Amazon distribution centre in Figure 12.

3 Summarise the benefits of the positive multiplier under these headings:
   Jobs   Earnings   Spending
   Image of the region.

4 **a)** Outline the main advantages and disadvantages of the growth of jobs in supermarkets and online retailing.
   b) Is the change from manufacturing to service jobs a good thing or not? Give reasons for your view.

Merthyr Tydfil — Employment change in Merthyr Tydfil

There have been major changes in employment in Merthyr Tydfil. A decline in 'heavy' manufacturing jobs saw the development of the Hoover factory in 1948. The factory, which made washing machines and tumble dryers, dominated employment in the town, providing over 5,000 jobs in the late twentieth century. Hoover is a multi-national company with its headquarters now in Italy. In 2009 the Hoover factory closed, with the decision to move the production of washing machines to Turkey where its costs would be lower.

As employment in Hoover declined there was a switch from manufacturing jobs to service sector jobs. The largest employers in Merthyr are now all in the service sector: the local council, the health service, a T-Mobile call centre, the Welsh Assembly and Tesco. As the nature of employment changes, people need re-training so that they can access other jobs. The Welsh Assembly Government provided regeneration funds to develop new skills and create new jobs. In Merthyr funds were used to build the leisure complex, enterprise centre, the WAG office and a retail park in which these service sector jobs are located.

The **de-industrialisation** of towns like Merthyr obviously creates major social consequences for local people.

Job losses may mean that families can no longer afford to make mortgage repayments. House repossessions and poverty both increased, especially in the valleys of South Wales, during the economic recession of 2008–9.

There have been two exceptions to de-industrialisation in Merthyr. The town is the favoured site for a huge new £400 million incinerator that would convert 750,000 tonnes of Welsh waste each year into electricity, creating 500 construction and 100 permanent jobs within the 'green' industry.

Also, a large opencast coal mine has been re-developed close to the town. The Ffos-y-Fran site opened in 2007. It is expected to produce 10 million tonnes of coal over seventeen years. The company running the mine claim that they will create 200 jobs directly at the site and that a further 400 people will gain extra work as a result of the operation of the mine. However, not everyone is happy. Some local people are concerned about noise and dust from the site which, at its closest, is only 40 m from homes. In August 2009 a protest camp was set up beside the mine. Climate change protesters argue that carbon dioxide from burning coal is a major cause of climate change and they want the site to close.

www.millerargent.co.uk
This website explains the environmental and community benefits of the Ffos-y-Fran opencast site.

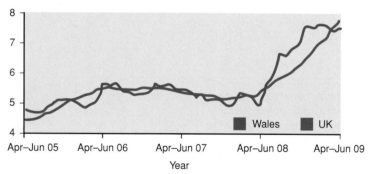

Figure 14 Changes in the unemployment rate, 2005–9

Figure 15 Opinions of the workers laid off from the Hoover plant

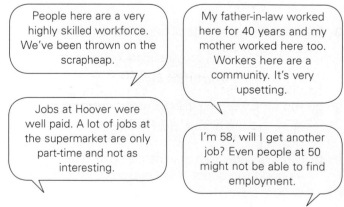

People here are a very highly skilled workforce. We've been thrown on the scrapheap.

My father-in-law worked here for 40 years and my mother worked here too. Workers here are a community. It's very upsetting.

Jobs at Hoover were well paid. A lot of jobs at the supermarket are only part-time and not as interesting.

I'm 58, will I get another job? Even people at 50 might not be able to find employment.

Activity

1 a) Describe how employment structure in Merthyr Tydfil is changing.
   b) Suggest two different reasons why patterns of work in Merthyr are changing.

2 Explain why workers at the Hoover plant were upset to lose their jobs.

3 a) Outline three different social problems that might be created by job losses.
   b) Suggest why the Welsh Assembly Government provided regeneration funds for Merthyr.

4 Outline the positive and negative impacts of the Ffos-y-Fran opencast site.

5 Research the Ffos-y-Fran website. This gives the point of view of the developer. Suggest the advantages and disadvantages of this development using these headings:

   Environmental impacts
   Social and economic impacts.

GIS Activity: The Poverty Site

Using GIS to investigate standard of living

www.poverty.org.uk/summary/maps.shtml

There are a growing number of online atlases that use Geographical Information Systems (GIS) to display data on maps. A GIS will allow you to interact with the data: you can select the data that interests you and display it in map or graph form. A screenshot from one such atlas is shown below. The atlas displays standard of living indicators such as low pay, unemployment or benefit claimants collected from local authorities in England, Scotland and Wales.

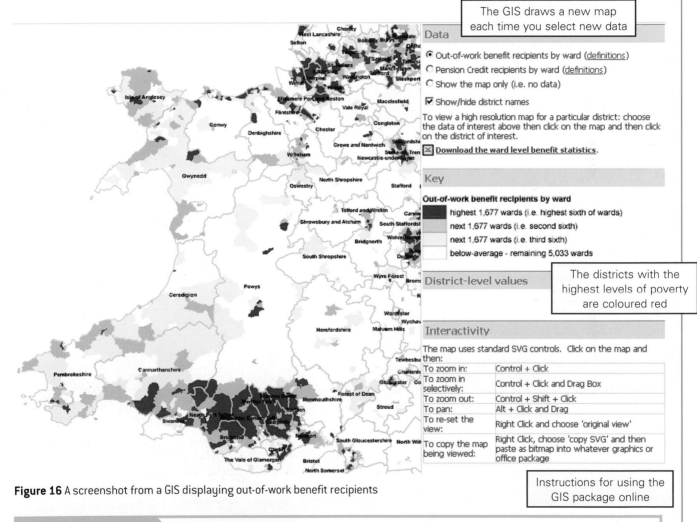

The GIS draws a new map each time you select new data

Data

- ● Out-of-work benefit recipients by ward (definitions)
- ○ Pension Credit recipients by ward (definitions)
- ○ Show the map only (i.e. no data)
- ☑ Show/hide district names

To view a high resolution map for a particular district: choose the data of interest above then click on the map and then click on the district of interest.

☒ **Download the ward level benefit statistics.**

Key

Out-of-work benefit recipients by ward

▉	highest 1,677 wards (i.e. highest sixth of wards)
▨	next 1,677 wards (i.e. second sixth)
▧	next 1,677 wards (i.e. third sixth)
▢	below-average - remaining 5,033 wards

District-level values

The districts with the highest levels of poverty are coloured red

Interactivity

The map uses standard SVG controls. Click on the map and then:

To zoom in:	Control + Click
To zoom in selectively:	Control + Click and Drag Box
To zoom out:	Control + Shift + Click
To pan:	Alt + Click and Drag
To re-set the view:	Right Click and choose 'original view'
To copy the map being viewed:	Right Click, choose 'copy SVG' and then paste as bitmap into whatever graphics or office package

Figure 16 A screenshot from a GIS displaying out-of-work benefit recipients

Instructions for using the GIS package online

Activity

1 Use Figure 16.
  a) Describe the distribution of districts where the number of out-of-work benefit recipients is highest.
  b) What evidence is there that the number of people out of work is higher or lower in rural districts?

2 Use the GIS weblink to investigate patterns of benefit recipients, low paid workers and premature deaths in your own region. Structure a short report around the following headings:
  Geographical patterns in the data
  Possible connections between the data.

How and why is farming in Wales changing?

Many farmers believe that livestock farming in the Less Favoured Area has become unsustainable. Farm incomes declined due to:

- disruption following foot and mouth disease
- imports of cheap lamb from New Zealand
- increased costs of feed, fertiliser and fuel.

This helps to explain why so many farmers have diversified their income.

'The beef and sheep farm was increasingly reliant on the EU Single Farm Payment so the decision was made to change to biofuel production by growing oilseed rape which is processed on the farm.' This was also a response to climate change and increasing fuel prices. There are three presses in a converted hay barn and the process also yields cake, which can be fed to cattle.

Local farmers opposed a new supermarket and offered an alternative – the Deli. 'We want to keep Pwllheli alive and give people the option to buy quality, local food. The shop is also a point where holidaymakers and urban people can come into contact with local farmers and we can communicate the story behind the food.'

Locally collected seed is used to grow native Welsh trees and shrubs. Young plants are provided for hedging schemes, shelter belts, roadside and woodland plantings across Wales, with bodies such as the National Trust, the RSPB, the Environment Agency, County Councils, schools and farmers among the customers.

From 2001 to 2009, 10 hectares of woodland were regenerated with 120,000 new trees, 5 km of hedgerow planted and 2 hectares of wetlands and ponds established. This reduced flooding as the new trees soak up water. The quality of rivers for fishing improved. The trees act as shelter belts for livestock, give new habitats for wildlife and provide a renewable supply of biomass, which can either be chipped and used as animal bedding, or for firewood. The trees absorb carbon dioxide from the atmosphere.

In 2006 a dairy farm began the Daioni range of organic flavoured milk drinks. In 2009 the business employed 20 people with clients including Welsh Rugby Union and Chelsea FC.

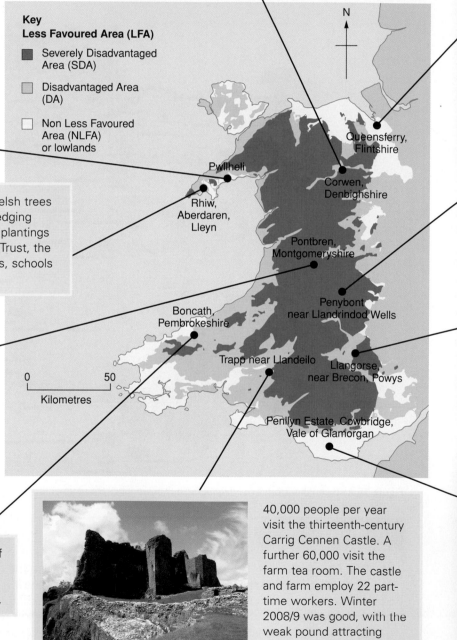

Key
Less Favoured Area (LFA)

- Severely Disadvantaged Area (SDA)
- Disadvantaged Area (DA)
- Non Less Favoured Area (NLFA) or lowlands

N

Queensferry, Flintshire

Corwen, Denbighshire

Pwllheli

Rhiw, Aberdaren, Lleyn

Pontbren, Montgomeryshire

Penybont near Llandrindod Wells

Boncath, Pembrokeshire

Trapp near Llandeilo

Llangorse, near Brecon, Powys

Penllyn Estate, Cowbridge, Vale of Glamorgan

0   50
Kilometres

40,000 people per year visit the thirteenth-century Carrig Cennen Castle. A further 60,000 visit the farm tea room. The castle and farm employ 22 part-time workers. Winter 2008/9 was good, with the weak pound attracting many visitors from the euro zone. Beef for the freezer from the quality Longhorn herd is sold at the farm shop. 'We've cut down on the sheep. We were chasing subsidies before.'

Figure 17 Examples of farm diversification in Wales

Leeks are grown for the Really Welsh Trading Company which also rents land from farmers to grow cauliflowers and daffodils in South Wales. Produce is packed in the field, with trimmings and unfit produce composted back into the soil, reducing transport costs and pollution. The firm was started in 2005 by a farmer who was fed up with producing crops for other people to brand them as their own. The farmer decided to launch his own brand, design his own packaging and sell directly to local supermarkets.

The business started with the purchase of a hedge trimmer for the tractor with contracts for highway and motorway verge mowing. This expanded by employing several local farmers' sons in: environmental maintenance for Powys; tree work, fencing and the control of weeds for the Highways Agency; dredging work for the Environment Agency; gates and marker posts showing signed rights of way.

A pony trekking and beef farm has changed by converting barns into rock climbing, abseiling and caving challenges. Outdoors there is an obstacle course, a dingle scramble and SkyTrek – a fast-moving glide system. There is camping and farmhouse accommodation.

Activity

1 Study Figure 17.
   a) Make a table similar to this:

Farm diversification			
Non-farming schemes	Schemes resulting from changing demands for food	Schemes to improve the countryside	Schemes directed at improving global environmental concerns

   b) Using the examples around the map, complete the columns with appropriate examples.

2 Go to www.reallywelsh.com. Describe this Welsh farming company. Why do you think it has been successful?

3 What patterns of diversification/change are found on farms near you? Contact local farmers or research from the web. Sites you could use include:
   Farming news section of the Western Mail:
   www.walesonline.co.uk/countryside-farming-news
   www.farmersguardian.com

Diversification ventures include: fly fishing, paintball games, timber processing, daffodils for medicine, miscanthus (elephant grass) for biofuel, green waste (grass and hedge cuttings and Christmas trees) from the council recycled for composting. **Extensification** (less intensive farming) with Tir Gofal.

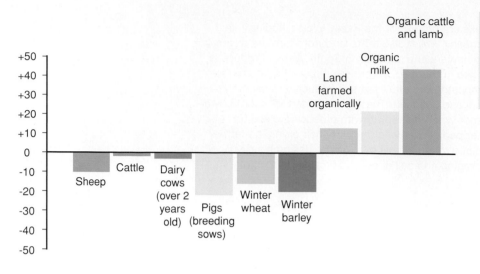

Figure 18 Changes in type of farming in Wales, 2007–8

How does employment change affect rural society?

The changes to rural employment have a number of social consequences. Some young people don't want to work on the family farm. They move away to get a job in the city. The result is an ageing rural population. Fewer families mean there is less demand for community services such as village shops, post offices, pubs and bus services, which results in them closing down.

Isolation and loneliness may be the result of a declining rural economy. If rural populations become too small then essential services such as schools and doctor's clinics become increasingly inefficient and expensive to sustain. If a doctor's surgery closes, local people find that they are further and further away from health care. Rural communities could become unsustainable and have no future.

The lack of **affordable housing** in rural areas is often linked to the sale of rural houses as second homes or holiday cottages. When a rural house is sold to be used as second home at weekends or during holidays, effects include:

1 One fewer house is available to local people. Increasing demand for rural homes forces up rural house prices.
2 Even more village services are likely to close. Second-home owners may only spend a few weeks of each year in the village, so have little use for local services.
3 The outward migration of rural Welsh-speaking families and inward migration of people from non-rural areas can reduce Welsh culture.

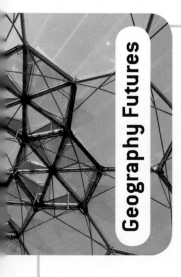

Geography Futures

Rural Development Plan for Wales for 2007 to 2013

This is a Welsh Assembly Government plan supported by European Union money to try to reduce the flow of people out of the rural areas of Wales. Nearly £800 million (WAG £600 million, EU £195 million) is to be invested in Welsh farming, forestry and rural communities. The grant money is to be spent on:

- Farming Connect – an internet scheme that provides advice on 'adding value to Welsh farm produce'.
- The expansion of agri-environment schemes which benefit wildlife, character of rural area, historic environment, increased public access, organic schemes such as Tir Gofal, Tir Cynnal, Tir Mynydd – a support scheme for the 'Less Favoured Areas'.
- Assisting the diversification of the rural economy, supporting business development and improving the quality of life in rural areas. One type of support is to improve broadband connection to allow more people to work from home and thus encourage people to live in rural areas.

If the measures to improve Welsh farming are not successful, the effects would be:

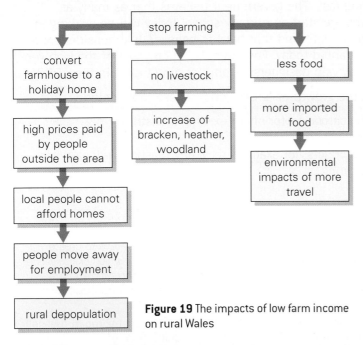

Figure 19 The impacts of low farm income on rural Wales

Activity

2 Use Figure 19 to outline the impacts of the changing nature of farming in Wales under the following headings:
   Social impacts on local people
   Impacts on the environment.

3 Read page 122 and describe the impacts of the sale of rural houses to holidaymakers.

4 Use the website www.homes4locals.com/index. html to investigate the strong opinions about how rural communities in Wales should be protected from further change.
   a) Use the site to outline:
      • the cause of the issue
      • what this pressure group thinks should be done.
   b) Do you agree with this point of view? Give your reasons.

GIS Activity: National Statistics

Using the National Statistics website to investigate population structure

www.statistics.gov.uk/census2001/pyramids/pages/W.asp

The National Statistics website is an official UK government site for the UK Census. The data has all sorts of population data and includes population pyramids for many regions of the UK. The link above will take you to the screen shown in Figure 20. Click on one of the links to a national level or an English region to view pyramids for other parts of the UK.

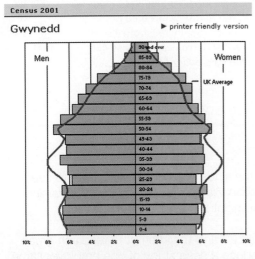

Figure 20 A screenshot showing the population pyramid for Gwynedd. Clicking on the links will allow you to view a new pyramid for each local authority in Wales

Activity

1 **a)** Compare the population pyramid of Gwynedd (shown by the bars) with that of the UK average.
   b) Suggest reasons for the lack of people in the 25–45 age group.

2 Use the population pyramids on the National Statistics site to investigate population structure in a variety of Welsh authorities. Investigate the following enquiry questions:
   a) Are there more retired people in coastal regions?
   b) Are there fewer young adults in rural authorities?

3 Suggest another enquiry question that you could investigate using these population pyramids.

Geography Futures

Future jobs in Wales

The world of work is changing fast. The government believes that as many as seven out of ten children who are starting primary school today will be working in jobs that haven't been invented yet! Find that hard to believe? Just consider some of the jobs that we take for granted today. For example, when you surf the web you are viewing pages designed by web designers: a job that didn't exist in the 1980s.

In the future WAG expects the growth of 'green jobs'. These jobs include:

- finding ways to reduce the carbon footprints of existing industries
- research into renewable energy
- changing waste into new products, for example recycling plastic, cardboard and steel waste from manufacturing.

We need to focus on manufacturing. An economy that doesn't make things can't generate enough money for families and public services. We need to develop a direction for manufacturing over the next ten years. We must do more to encourage people to create new businesses in Wales as well as attract investment. We must identify which skills will be required in the world over the next ten years. We must look at skills for the future, to be ahead of the game. We need to gear our education system towards improving those skills. We need jobs based on high skills not low wages.

We must look to develop green jobs. We can do this. Already we have a hydrogen fuel-cell cluster. We need to ensure that everybody can see the opportunities in the new technologies. Green jobs are sustainable jobs. New ways of generating power create new opportunities for job creation.

Figure 21 Carwyn Jones, Welsh First Minister, speaking in 2009

Green changes have been made by Corus in Port Talbot steelworks to reduce the amount of energy they use. Carbon dioxide emissions have also been reduced by re-using gas generated inside the plant.

Green jobs in Wales

Sharp in Wrexham produces solar modules for the European market.

In 2008, Ford invested £70 million in its engine plant at Bridgend, South Wales, to produce a new generation of petrol engines that will provide up to 20 per cent better fuel economy and 15 per cent lower carbon dioxide emissions. This helped to secure the plant's future for its 2,000 employees.

Sims, Newport, is the biggest metal recycling plant in the UK. A unit processing waste from electrical and electronic equipment opened in 2009. Computers and computer equipment which cannot be re-used are also reprocessed by separating out copper, aluminium and plastic which are then sold on. The facility is built near to Sims' existing shredder and fridge recycling facility in the South Docks area of the city. Scrap metal is delivered, by rail, from 29 UK sites to a giant shredder, which can process 450 end-of-life cars every hour.

Figure 22 Examples of green jobs in Wales

Activity

1 Suggest why the Welsh Assembly First Minister thinks that:
   a) Wales will need manufacturing jobs in the future
   b) high-level skills are more important than low wages.

2 Discuss the kinds of jobs you would like to see developed in Wales. Outline the kinds of training/skills that might be needed for these jobs.

3 Use Figure 22 and the internet to research green jobs. Produce a case study of one employer (large or small) that is creating a greener future.

What changes are likely to take place in energy supply and demand in Wales?

How does Wales supply its current energy needs?

We need energy to light and heat our homes, schools and offices and to provide power in our factories. We also need energy for transport. Due to the remoteness of many rural regions, only 44 per cent of homes in Wales have mains gas for heating. The production of electricity is therefore essential. Wales produces most of its electrical energy by burning **fossil fuels**. A much smaller percentage comes from renewable sources. However, the physical environment of Wales, with its mountains and rivers, and coastline with a large tidal range, make it suitable for the further development of several types of renewable energy such as wind, hydro, tidal and wave power.

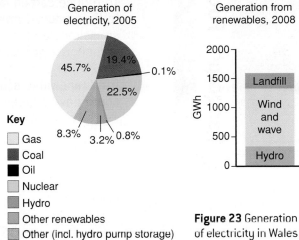

Generation of electricity, 2005

45.7% 19.4% 0.1% 22.5% 8.3% 3.2% 0.8%

Key
☐ Gas
■ Coal
■ Oil
☐ Nuclear
☐ Hydro
☐ Other renewables
☐ Other (incl. hydro pump storage)

Generation from renewables, 2008

Landfill
Wind and wave
Hydro

Figure 23 Generation of electricity in Wales

Figure 25 Energy in the UK

a Changing demand, 1998–2008 (100,000 tonnes of oil equivalent)

	1998	2004	2008
Total demand	169.0	172.0	165.0
Iron and steel	4.0	1.7	1.7
Other industries	30.5	31.3	28.6
Transport	53.8	57.7	58.2
Domestic	46.1	48.6	45.9
Commercial	9.7	10.0	9.8
Other	21.5	20.3	19.3

b 2008 energy consumption (%) compared with 2007

Total	**−0.5**
Domestic sector	+3.1
Industrial sector	−3.3
Service sector	+2.4
Transport sector	−2.2

Key
■ Coal-fired
■ Gas-fired
■ Gas-fired due to open 2012

Connah's Quay Deeside

Baglan Bay Uskmouth
Aberthaw B Barry

N

0 50
Kilometres

Figure 24 Location of coal- and gas-fired power stations in Wales, 2010

Activity

1 Use Figure 23.
   a) What was the total renewable contribution to the supply of electricity in 2005?
   b) Describe the different levels of contribution of each of the renewables in 2008.

2 a) Describe the distribution of coal- and gas-fired power stations in Wales as shown in Figure 24.
   b) Research the positive and negative impacts of the liquid natural gas terminal and pipeline.

3 Study Figure 25.
   a) Which uses of energy are expanding? Which are reducing?
   b) Describe the trends shown. Suggest why the total demand for energy reduced during the period 2004–8.

4 Why is Wales well-suited to producing renewable energy (wind, tide, wave, hydro) as near the consumer as possible?

Future renewable energy sources in Wales

The burning of coal, gas and oil produces carbon dioxide, a major greenhouse gas. To reduce carbon dioxide emissions, WAG has set targets for more energy in Wales to be produced from renewable sources. This would reduce the carbon dioxide emissions that come from energy production. Its target is: 3 per cent reduction in greenhouse gas emissions each year from 2011 onwards. The 2020 EU target is for 20 per cent of energy requirements (electricity, heat and vehicle fuels) to come from renewable sources. Read the suggestions on these pages to see how Wales could have a greener, low-carbon future.

	Carbon dioxide emissions
Production of electricity (from gas and coal)	4.0
Other energy uses (e.g. gas for heating, petrol and diesel for transport)	5.5
Non-energy emissions (including agriculture and waste management)	2.5
Total	12.0

Figure 26 Carbon dioxide emissions for Wales 2007 (MtC of greenhouse gas a year)

Biomass energy

Wales aims to increase the use of **biomass** for energy. This will be through planting more forest and energy crops (willow) or energy grasses (miscanthus). However, too much development would mean less land available for other agriculture.

A paper plant at Shotton and a £400 million 'Prenergy' development at Port Talbot are industries using biomass.

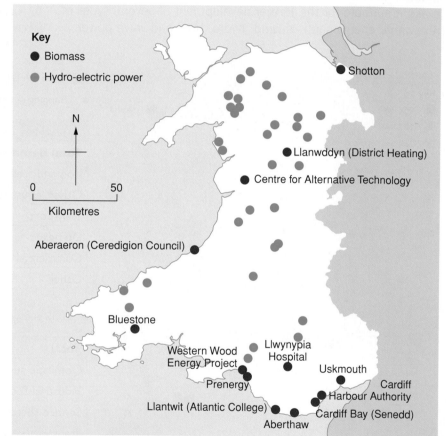

Figure 27 Biomass and HEP (2007 data)

Hydro-electric power

In 2005 the pump storage hydro schemes at Dinorwig and Blaenau Ffestiniog generated approximately 85 per cent of the **hydro-electricity** in Wales. The development of large amounts of new hydro-power in Wales is not possible because most suitable sites are already used. However, there is development of smaller hydro schemes as community projects, for example at Aber below Talybont Reservoir.

Energy from waste

As landfill sites become full, businesses are charged high costs for disposing of their waste. Instead there has been development of large incinerators to create energy from waste. In 2009 Covanta Energy, an American company, proposed a £400 million incinerator sited in Merthyr Tydfil to convert 0.75 million tonnes of waste annually, into electricity for 180,000 homes.

Marine

Wales has a great potential to exploit power from the sea. It is suggested that more than half the current electricity consumption could come from tide and wave projects by 2025. Possible projects include: the Severn Barrage which could provide 5 per cent of UK electricity; E.ON/Lunar tidal stream and Wave Dragon wave-power projects sites off Pembrokeshire; Anglesey tidal stream; and tidal lagoons at Rhyl; Upper Severn.

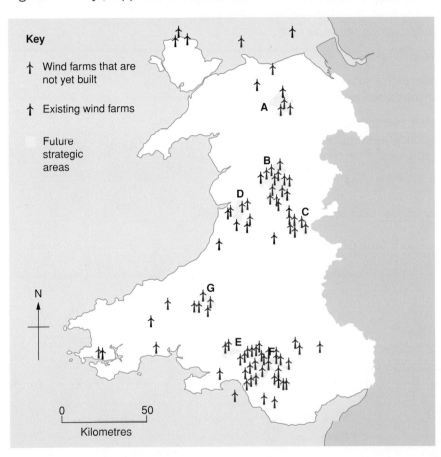

Key

↑ Wind farms that are not yet built

↑ Existing wind farms

Future strategic areas

N

0 ——— 50
Kilometres

Figure 28 Wind farms (2007 data)

Wind

In 2009, 300 MW were generated from onshore wind turbines and 60 MW from one offshore wind farm at North Hoyle. That's enough for about 33,500 homes. Most wind farms in Wales are small, with fewer than ten turbines, but there are twenty larger sites that each produce enough electricity for more than 1,000 homes.

In 2007, seven areas in Wales were identified as the most appropriate locations for larger-scale wind farms (see Figure 28). If all these projects go ahead, wind farms could create almost a third of Wales' electricity demand by 2015. Offshore, proposals for two large wind farms –750 MW off Abergele in North Wales and 1,500 MW in the outer Bristol Channel near Lundy – would provide nearly a sixth of Wales' energy demand.

Development of other energy sources

Research and development of solar panels and solar photovoltaic electric cells in north-east Wales are helping to bring down the high cost of solar energy. New technology for existing power stations is also being developed, for example the 2008 £8 million npower carbon capture scheme at Aberthaw B power station, South Wales.

Activity

1 Read the following statements:

'We now need to look radically at the options and resources available to us …'

'Your responses will enable us to prepare … an action plan as well as informing our wider climate change and energy related work.'
Welsh Assembly Government 2008

2 Using the information on these two pages and on pages 128–132, write to the Energy Minister responding to this consultation. Give your opinion on which energy sources should be used in the future.
   a) Start your letter with a summary of advantages and disadvantages of renewable and non-renewable sources of energy.
   b) State the targets required by government.
   c) In your opinion, what type(s) of energy source should be developed? Give the reasons for your decisions.

What conflicts of opinion are created by new sources of energy?

Gwynt-Y-Môr (Windy Sea), Llandudno – offshore wind farm

The proposed Gwynt y Môr offshore wind farm in North Wales would be Wales' largest wind farm. It would produce more than ten times more energy than the existing offshore wind farm at North Hoyle. The project involves the construction offshore of:

- 200 wind turbines, each 165 m tall and generating a maximum of 3–5 megawatts
- underwater power cables to take the electricity from the wind turbines to the shore
- 3–5 meteorological masts for weather data to operate the wind farm.

It also involves construction work on land to provide:

- underground power cables to an onshore electricity substation
- 500 m of overhead power cables from the substation to existing overhead lines.

However, the scale of the development is controversial. During the consultation phase a number of stakeholders expressed concern, so npower modified their plans. The new farm covers a smaller area to give:

- a wider shipping lane to the north and south of the wind farm
- a narrower view of the wind turbines
- more room for helicopters approaching the adjacent Douglas oil and gas platform.

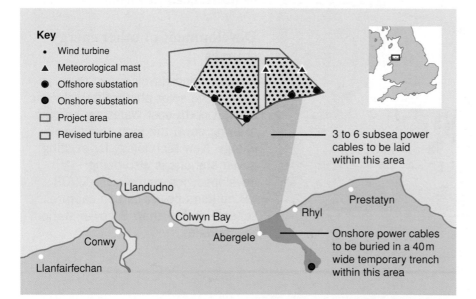

Figure 29 Gwynt y Môr

Figure 30 Arguments in favour of the proposal

This new offshore wind farm would create enough power every year for 40 per cent of the homes in Wales. It would mean that Wales was leading the way on this technology and make the UK the world's biggest producer of offshore renewable power, creating thousands of new jobs.

npower

Gwynt y Môr should be built as it will generate a tenth of Wales' electricity consumption and prevent the emission of 2 million tonnes of carbon dioxide each year. Climate change is the biggest threat we face this century and we have to be taking action now.
We do not believe that the wind farm will harm tourism. In a similar situation, the council at Great Yarmouth has found that the wind farm just 3 km from their shoreline has benefited tourism.

Friends of the Earth Cymru

Figure 31 Arguments against the proposal

David Bellamy hits out at North Wales wind farm plans

Botanist David Bellamy hit out at 'wind vandals' who will trash the North Wales coast unless the building of Britain's second largest wind farm off the coast of Llandudno is blocked. 'The sums just don't add up and if we're not careful we will destroy what we want to preserve, the North Wales landscape and lifestyles, with a headlong rush into a flawed technology which will cause serious social, landscape and visual harm, produce a small amount of intermittent electricity and cost the taxpayer billions of pounds in unnecessary subsidy.'

Decision-making powers for larger offshore wind farms lie with the Westminster government. Planning permission was granted earlier this month. 'We've got devolution now, but they've gone right over our heads and ignored the Assembly, town councils and the will of local people.'

The company has up to five years before it has to start work on the site. Developers npower could sell off up to half of its interest in the £2.2bn scheme to spread costs in tough economic times. Any uncertainty over the future of the wind farm, eight miles from Llandudno, could hit property prices in the area.

Source: the *Daily Post*, 16 December 2008

Figure 32 The view out to sea from Llandudno

Activity

1   Look at the websites of the following organisations and companies: npower, Friends of the Earth and SOS.

2   Argue the case for and against the Gwynt y Môr wind farm. Should the wind farm be built? Give, with reasons, your own view.

www.saveourscenery.com/index.html
The 'What you need to know' section gives information on visual and noise pollution. It describes possible economic impacts. There are links to three YouTube videos.
A video of the 2009 decision about the wind farm can be found at:
www.dailypost.co.uk/videos-pics/videos/news-videos/2009/01/08/gwynt-y-m-r-wind-farm-decision-55578-22646711

Geography Futures

Should we have tidal power in the Severn estuary?

The Severn estuary has the second highest tidal range (the difference between high and low water) in the world. Water flows rapidly in and out of the estuary with each tide. For many years there have been different proposals to generate power from these tides. In January 2009 five options for tidal power were chosen for further review.

Generating the power   How a lagoon system works

1 At high tide turbine gates are open

Seaward side

Landward side

2 Allowing sea water to flow through turbines, generating electricity and filling lagoon

Landward side

Seaward side

3 At low tide the process is reversed

3 Onshore lagoon on Welsh side (Fleming lagoon)
- Would provide 0.75 per cent of UK electricity demand
- Construction cost £4.1–£4.9 billion
- May have less effect on local ports and fisheries than barrages
- 6,500 hectares intertidal habitat loss, lower impact on intertidal habitat than large barrage
- Possible build-up of sediment within the impounded area

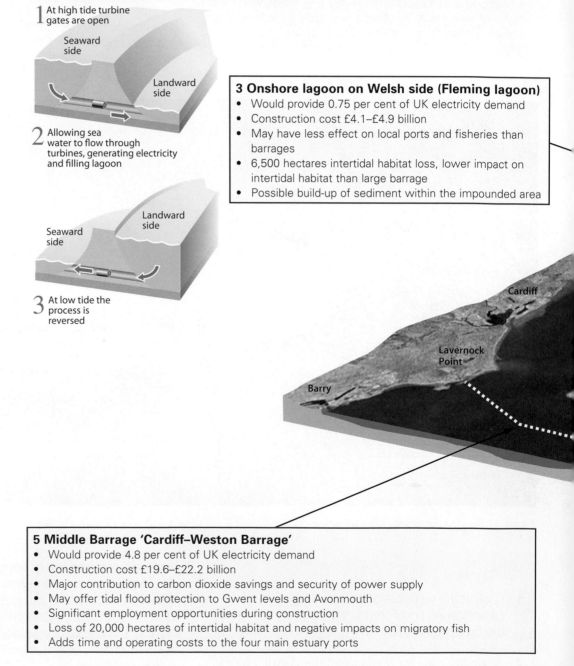

Cardiff

Lavernock Point

Barry

5 Middle Barrage 'Cardiff–Weston Barrage'
- Would provide 4.8 per cent of UK electricity demand
- Construction cost £19.6–£22.2 billion
- Major contribution to carbon dioxide savings and security of power supply
- May offer tidal flood protection to Gwent levels and Avonmouth
- Significant employment opportunities during construction
- Loss of 20,000 hectares of intertidal habitat and negative impacts on migratory fish
- Adds time and operating costs to the four main estuary ports

Figure 33 The five options for tidal power, January 2009

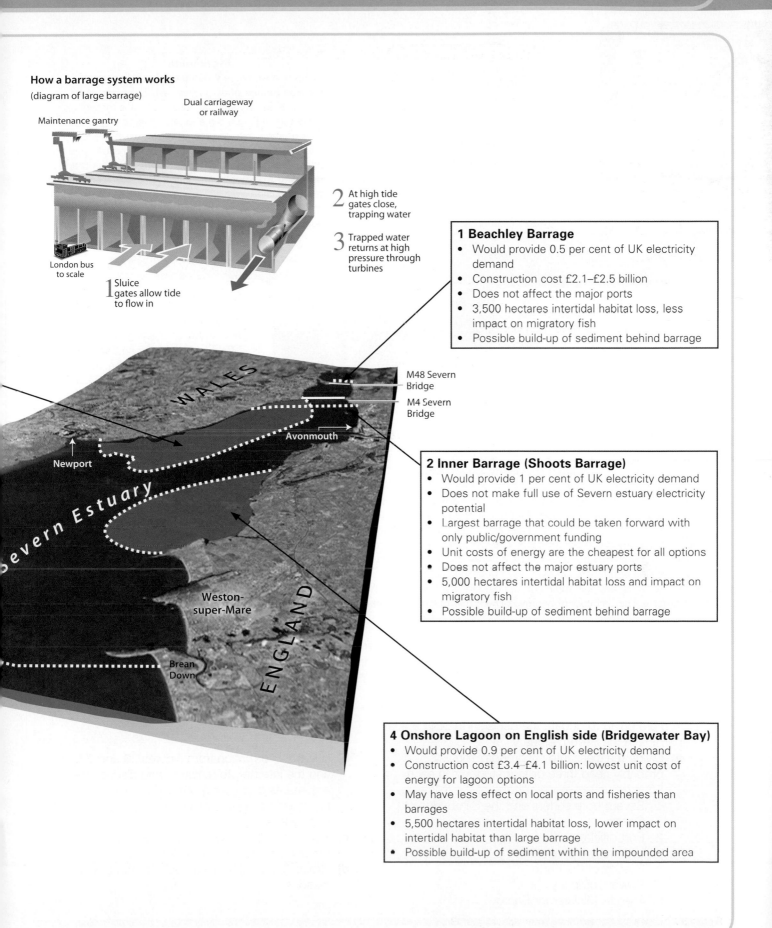

How a barrage system works

(diagram of large barrage)

Maintenance gantry

Dual carriageway
or railway

London bus
to scale

2 At high tide
gates close,
trapping water

3 Trapped water
returns at high
pressure through
turbines

1 Sluice
gates allow tide
to flow in

M48 Severn
Bridge

M4 Severn
Bridge

WALES

Avonmouth

Newport

Severn Estuary

Weston-
super-Mare

Brean
Down

ENGLAND

1 Beachley Barrage
- Would provide 0.5 per cent of UK electricity demand
- Construction cost £2.1–£2.5 billion
- Does not affect the major ports
- 3,500 hectares intertidal habitat loss, less impact on migratory fish
- Possible build-up of sediment behind barrage

2 Inner Barrage (Shoots Barrage)
- Would provide 1 per cent of UK electricity demand
- Does not make full use of Severn estuary electricity potential
- Largest barrage that could be taken forward with only public/government funding
- Unit costs of energy are the cheapest for all options
- Does not affect the major estuary ports
- 5,000 hectares intertidal habitat loss and impact on migratory fish
- Possible build-up of sediment behind barrage

4 Onshore Lagoon on English side (Bridgewater Bay)
- Would provide 0.9 per cent of UK electricity demand
- Construction cost £3.4–£4.1 billion: lowest unit cost of energy for lagoon options
- May have less effect on local ports and fisheries than barrages
- 5,500 hectares intertidal habitat loss, lower impact on intertidal habitat than large barrage
- Possible build-up of sediment within the impounded area

Geography Futures

The highest spring tides produce the Severn Bore, a large wave that moves up the river. A barrage will stop the bore.

Record holder for surfing Severn Bore – 12 km

Avonmouth
The port employs 7,500 people, dealing with 12 million tonnes of cargo per year. The barrage will slow down ships as they queue to move through. Unless the locks are big enough for large ships, the number of ships able to reach the port will be reduced. Avonmouth is closer to a central position in the UK than any other port. Transport by ship into the port saves hundreds of kilometres of road and rail transport. Ships are ten times more carbon dioxide efficient than other modes of transport. A barrage only generates electricity for six hours a day in two bursts, once on each tide. The time of the tide might not coincide with the peak demand for electricity.

We need all the carbon-free electricity we can get but there are other ways without building a large structure in the Severn estuary. This could be by: 1) increasing nuclear power and 2) research into technology that captures carbon from coal-fired stations, and into sites where the carbon could be buried.

Power company

Construction of the Cardiff–Weston Barrage would take ten years, with a 10 million tonne carbon footprint. It would generate new traffic on existing road networks in rural areas and around Cardiff airport.
The barrage project cannot be justified on flood protection grounds. Flood defence schemes can be built quickly and sea-level rises take decades. Tidal lagoons built a mile offshore should be chosen. These store a head of water and create power from both the ebb and flow of the tide.

Friends of the Earth Cymru

Cardiff University, Engineering
South Wales and Devon have to import energy. The UK needs a wide variety of 'local' energy sources. A barrage will provide carbon-free energy and we will not be dependent on other countries for our power.
The calmer water in the reduced tidal range above the barrage will mean more deposition of mud and clearer conditions which will encourage more fish. This will attract more birds but they will be different from those currently in the area. The new idea of offshore lagoons may affect the ecosystem the least but there is little research on their impact on the estuary, its wildlife and the industries it supports. The unit cost of energy is twice that of land-connected lagoons.

Slimbridge Wildfowl and Wetlands Centre
70,000 waterbirds are dependent on the wetland area. Geese graze on the intertidal meadow. A barrage would reduce the range of the tide. There would be less grazing area for birds.

Figure 34 Opinions on the options for tidal energy from the Severn estuary. The photo shows Slimbridge Wildfowl and Wetlands Centre

Activity

1 You are going to debate the decision to build a tidal barrage in the Severn estuary.
   a) Divide the class into six groups. You will probably need three or four students in each. Each group will represent one of the following:
   1 Severn bore surfers and the Slimbridge Centre
   2 Port officials
   3 University engineers
   4 Friends of the Earth
   5 Power company
   6 The UK Minister for Energy

   b) Use the information from Figures 33 and 34, and the internet, to research and discuss the arguments that your group will put forward at the meeting. You should prepare to speak for two minutes.
   c) Hold the debate. Allow each of groups 1–5 to make a statement. Group 6 can ask questions.
   d) Group 6 should make a decision and give its reasons.

Glossary

A

Agri-business – Farming combined with commercial activities to maximise production and profits.

Affordable housing – Houses that are either sold or rented at relatively low cost.

Anticyclone – An area of high pressure in the atmosphere associated with dry, settled periods of weather.

Air mass – A large parcel of air in the atmosphere. All parts of the air mass have similar temperature and moisture content at ground level.

Aspect – The direction in which a slope or other feature faces.

B

Backwash – The flow of water back into the sea after a wave has broken on a beach.

Barrier reef – A long structure in the sea, parallel to the coast, built of limestone by millions of corals.

Beach replenishment – Adding extra sand or gravel to a beach to make it wider and thicker.

Biodiversity hotspot – A region with a particularly great variety of organisms. Central America is one such hotspot.

Biomass – Fuel that is used to generate electricity, or for heating/cooking, that is made from plant material.

Biomes – Ecosystems that exist at a very large scale (for example, tropical rainforests or deserts).

Breakwater – A form of hard engineering used as a coastal defence against erosion. Breakwaters may be built from granite blocks or angular pieces of concrete.

Brownfield site – A development site where older buildings are demolished or renovated before a new development takes place.

Budget airline – A company that offers cheap flights.

C

Climate – Taking weather readings over long periods of time, and then working out averages, patterns and trends.

Clone towns – Towns which have very few independently owned shops are sometimes referred to as 'clone towns'. This is because high streets which are full of chain stores, and have very few locally owned shops, have no local character and look the same (or are 'clones' of) every other high street.

Commercial logging – The cutting down of forests for the sale of their timber.

Culled – When an agreed number of animals is killed in order to control the growth of their population.

D

De-industrialisation – A shift in jobs from the manufacturing sector to jobs that provide a service.

Debt-for-nature-swap – An agreement between poorer nations that owe money to richer nations. The poorer nation agrees to spend money on a conservation project. In exchange the richer country agrees to cancel part of the debt of money that it is owed.

Deforestation – The cutting down or burning of trees.

Deposit – The laying down of material in the landscape. Deposition occurs when the force that was carrying the sediment is reduced.

Depression (economic) – A period of time in which the economy of a country is in decline. The usual effect of depression is greater unemployment.

Depression (weather) – A weather system associated with low air pressure. Depressions bring changeable weather that includes rain and windy conditions.

Diversify – To create a wider variety of job opportunities.

Drought – A long period of time with little precipitation.

E

Ecosystem – A community of plants and animals and the environment in which they live. Ecosystems includes both living parts (e.g. plants) and non-living parts (e.g. air and water). Ecosystems exist at various scales from **biomes** such as rainforests to micro-scale ecosystems such as garden ponds.

Ecotourism – Small scale tourist projects that create money for conservation as well as creating local jobs

Employment structure – The number of people working in the primary, secondary and tertiary sectors of the economy.

Environmental refugees – People who are forced to leave their homes as a result of some environmental disaster. It is expected that sea level rise due to climate change will create millions of such refugees.

Erosion – The wearing away of the landscape.

Exports – The sale of products from one country to another.

Extensification – A change in the way that farm land is used. Less intensive land use that is better for wildlife.

F

Fetch – The distance a wave travels over open sea.

Glossary

Fjord – A deep water sea inlet in the coastline. These steep sided valleys are eroded by ice action.

Fossil fuels – Oil, coal or gas that is burnt to generate electricity or energy.

G

Greenhouse effect – A natural process in which gases such as carbon dioxide trap heat energy in the atmosphere.

Groundwater – Water in the ground below the water table.

H

Hard engineering – Artificial structures such as sea walls or concrete river embankments. They are constructed to try to control a natural process such as a river flood or coastal erosion.

Heatwave – A long period of hot weather that causes stress for animals, plants and people.

High-tech industry – The use of advanced technology in manufacturing such as defence systems and medical equipment.

Honeypot site – A place of special interest that attracts many tourists and is often congested at peak times.

Hydraulic action – Erosion caused when a wave forces water and air into gaps in rock or soil.

Hydro-electricity – Electricity generated by water flowing through turbines. Also known as hydro-electric power (HEP).

I

Illegal logging – The cutting down of forests for their timber by people who do not own the land or do not have the legal right to sell the timber.

Imports – The purchase of goods from another country.

Indigenous people – Tribal groups who are native to a particular place.

Intercepts – When water is prevented from falling directly to the ground. For example, the canopy of leaves in a forest intercepts rainfall.

K

Key services – The way in which ecosystems provide benefits for people. For example, mangrove forests act as coastal buffers, soaking up wave energy during a storm and reducing the risk of erosion and flooding.

Knowledge economy – Jobs that require high levels of education or training.

Knowledge-intensive industry – Jobs which require high levels of education or training.

L

Landslide – The sudden collapse of soil and rock from a slope.

Leaching – The removal of nutrients from the soil by water flowing through it.

Legacy – A development which provides benefits for the local community for many years to come.

Less Favoured Area (LFA) – Areas that receive special funding from the European Union.

Long-haul – A flight to a distant place.

Longshore drift – A process by which beach material Is moved along the coast.

M

Managed realignment – A coastal management strategy in which land is lost to the sea in a controlled way. Flooding of the existing sea defences is allowed and a new coastline established further inland.

Mangrove – A type of tropical forest that grows in coastal regions.

Mass tourism – A style of tourist development in which massive numbers of holiday makers are encouraged to visit a large resort. Mass tourism was used to create jobs along the Spanish Mediterranean coastline and at Cancun, Mexico among other places.

Mechanisation – The increased use of machines to replace human labour.

Multi-National Companies (MNCs) – Large businesses such as Sony, Microsoft and McDonalds, who have branches in several countries. Multi-national companies are also known as **trans-national companies (TNCs)**.

N

Net out-migration – When more people move into the region than leave it.

Nutrient cycle – The flow of nutrients between different stores in an ecosystem which forms a continuous chain (or cycle).

Nutrient flows – The movement of minerals from one store to another.

Nutrient stores – Parts of an ecosystem, such as the soil, in which nutrients are kept.

O

Offshore bar – A feature on the sea bed formed by the deposition of sand.

Glossary

P

Positive multiplier effect – A positive chain of events triggered by the creation of new jobs in a region.

Postglacial rebound – An adjustment in the level of the Earth's crust. The crust was depressed by the mass of ice lying on it during glacial periods of the ice age. Since the end of the last glacial period the crust has been slowly rising back to its original level.

Private sector – People who are either self employed or work for a larger company or organisation that is not controlled by the government.

Public sector – People employed by the national, regional or local government.

R

Recharge – Water that enters an aquifer and refills a groundwater store.

Relief rainfall – Precipitation that is caused when warm, moist air is forced to rise over a mountainous region. As the air rises it cools and the water vapour condenses forming rain clouds. Relief rainfall is also known as orographic rain.

Remote sensing – Collecting geographical data from a distance. For example, satellites orbiting the earth are used to collect data about weather systems.

Retreat – The gradual backward movement of a landform due to the process of erosion. The coastline retreats due to the erosion of a cliff and a waterfall retreats towards the source of a river as it is eroded.

Rural depopulation – When the population of a rural region decreases.

S

Sahel – The semi-arid region of North Africa to the south of the Sahara desert. The word means 'shore' in Arabic.

Sea wall – A form of hard engineering used as a coastal defence against erosion and flooding.

Shanty housing – Homes built by the residents themselves on land that they do not own.

Short-haul – A flight to a nearby destination. Short-haul flights from the UK either fly to other UK airports or to airports in the rest of Europe.

Shoreline Management Plan – The plan that details how a local authority will manage each stretch of coastline in the UK in the future.

Soft engineering – Alternative method of reducing floods by planting trees or allowing areas to flood naturally.

Solar footprint – The amount of the sun's energy that heats each square metre of the earth varies depending on latitude. Near the equator the sun hits the earth at almost 90°. The solar footprint is small and the amount of energy received per square metre is much greater than near to the poles.

Solar radiation – Heat and light energy from the sun. Solar radiation also includes other parts of the electro-magnetic spectrum such as ultra-violet and x-rays.

Spit – A coastal landform formed by the deposition of sediment in a low mound where the coastline changes direction, for example, at the mouth of a river.

Store – A place where something remains for a period of time e.g. within the water cycle or carbon cycle.

Storm surge – The rise in sea level that can cause coastal flooding during a storm or hurricane. The surge is due to a combination of two things. First, the low air pressure means that sea level can rise. Second, the strong winds can force a bulge of water on to the shoreline.

Subsidence – The sinking of land. Subsidence may be due to natural processes, such as the compaction of sediment in a delta, or the thawing of permafrost. At other times subsidence is due to human activity, such as the collapse of old mine workings underground.

Swash – The flow of water up the beach as a wave breaks on the shore.

Synoptic chart – A map that uses symbols to show a weather forecast.

T

Tombolo – A coastal landform made by deposition of sediment joining the coast to an island.

Tourist enclave – A tourist resort that is separated from local communities. Some tourist developments are designed so that tourists are discouraged from leaving the hotel or resort. In this way, the tourist spends more money with the company, and very little with local businesses.

Trans-National Companies (TNCs) – Large businesses such as Sony, Microsoft and McDonalds, who have branches in several countries. Trans-national companies are also known as **multi-national companies (MNCs)**.

Tropical rainforest – Large forest ecosystems (or biomes) that exist in the hot, wet climate found on either side of the equator.

Tundra – An ecosystem largely found in the Arctic region. The tundra is treeless because the growing season is short and the average monthly temperature is below 10 celsius.

Glossary

U

Unsustainable – Improving the lives of people but in a way that is using up too many natural resources and/or is polluting the environment so badly that future generations will have a lower quality of life.

W

Water cycle – The continuous flow of water between the earth's surface and the atmosphere – also called the hydrological cycle.

Wave-cut notch – A slot with overhanging rocks that has been cut into the bottom of a cliff by wave action.

Wave-cut platform – A coastal landform made of rocky shelf in front of a cliff. The wave cut platform is caused by erosion and left by the retreat of the cliff.

Weather – Features such as temperature, rainfall, cloud cover, and wind as they are experienced. Measurements of these features can be recorded over long periods of time and averages calculated. These averages are what we call **climate**.

Wilderness – Areas that have been left in a wild state. Wilderness regions are uninhabited and are not farmed. Large parts of Iceland can be described as wilderness.

Wildlife corridor – Strips of habitat that allow wild animals to migrate from one ecosystem to another. For example, wildlife corridors can be created by planting hedgerows and trees to connect remaining fragments of forest together.

Index

Index